Small Miracles
for
Families

Extraordinary Coincidences
That Reaffirm Our Deepest Ties

Yitta Halberstam
&
Judith Leventhal

ADAMS MEDIA CORPORATION
Avon, Massachusetts

We believe your family is another in life's miracles!

With love,

The Beal's

2007

Published by
Adams Media Corporation
57 Littlefield Street, Avon, MA 02322 U.S.A.
www.adamsmedia.com
ISBN 13: 978-1-58062-656-9
ISBN 10: 1-58062-656-4

Printed in Canada.

J I H G F E D C B

Library of Congress Cataloging-in-Publication Data
Mandelbaum, Yitta Halberstam.
Small miracles for families / Yitta Halberstam and Judith Leventhal.
p.   cm.
ISBN 1-58062-656-4
1. Family--Anecdotes. 2. Conduct of life--Anecdotes.
3. Coincidence--Psychic aspects. I. Leventhal, Judith, 1958- II. Title.

HQ734M2683 2003
306.87--dc21

2003002610

This publication is designed to provide accurate and authoritative information with regard to
the subject matter covered. It is sold with the understanding that the publisher is not engaged
in rendering legal, accounting, or other professional advice. If legal advice or other expert
assistance is required, the services of a competent professional person should be sought.
—From a *Declaration of Principles* jointly adopted by a Committee of the American Bar
Association and a Committee of Publishers and Associations

Many of the designations used by manufacturers and sellers to distinguish their products
are claimed as trademarks. Where those designations appear in this book and Adams
Media was aware of a trademark claim, the designations have been printed with initial
capital letters.

While all the stories in this book are true, some of the names, dates, and places have been
changed to protect anonymity.

Illustration © David David Gallery, Philadelphia / Superstock.

*This book is available at quantity discounts for bulk purchases.
For information, call 1-800-289-0963.*

Dedication

In loving memory of Claire Halberstam
and Anne Leventhal.

Permissions

Grateful acknowledgment is made to the following for permission to reprint previously published material:

The story on pages 66–71 is reprinted with permission from the *London Daily Mail*, Sunday, December 23, 2001, by Steven Steward, "If this wasn't a miracle, what was it?"

The story on pages 96–102 is reprinted with permission from *Health Magazine*, December 2001, page 76.

The story on pages 163–167 is reprinted with permission from the *Atlanta Journal Constitution*, November 3, 2000, by Bill Hendrick, page E1, "A Dying Wish Fulfilled Nearly Six Decades Later."

Acknowledgments

The past year has been a heartrending one for us. Yitta's mother—Claire Halberstam—passed away on April 24, 2002, of a heart attack; this occurred only two days after Judith's mother-in-law—Anne Leventhal—died following a year-long battle with cancer. We grieved simultaneously, but at different locations. Our hearts were wrenched by our mutual devastating losses.

As this is a book about families, we wish first and foremost to acknowledge the deep debts we owed these women for their love, loyalty, and devotion, and for their ever-constant enthusiasm and excitement about the *Small Miracles* series. The void is very big and deep without them, and we miss them very much. Now that they are no longer with us, we see many strengths and qualities in them that ironically we failed to recognize and appreciate while they were still alive.

We therefore are fervent in our hope that this book will bring to our cherished readers an understanding of the pivotal and irreplaceable role family members play in our everyday lives. Please revel in family warmth, nurture it, and recognize it for all its value and beauty, while it is still yours to keep. You never know when it can suddenly— and irrevocably—be taken away and forever lost.

Fortunately, we are blessed with many family members who, thank God, are still very much present in our daily lives. And to them, we offer our love and appreciation.

Yitta thanks: my wonderful in-laws, Rabbi Leib and Sima Mandelbaum, for their heartfelt devotion all these years; and my beloved brother Moishe and sister Miriam Halberstam, whom I love and appreciate more each passing day. A special note of appreciation to Miriam for her tremendous assistance in scouting for amazing stories and for her extraordinary publicity efforts—you're the best! Thanks also to my sisters and brothers-in-law, Suri and Danny Dymshitz; Chayie and Yeruchem Winkler; Baila and Chaim Mandelbaum; and Evelyn Halberstam for their support and assistance. Motty, my husband, you are my teacher, my mentor, and my pillar of strength; and my beloved children, Yossi and Eli: You give meaning and value to my life and bring me such happiness and pride—I cherish you so much and thank God every day for your blessing.

Judith thanks: my mother, Rose Frankel, and my father of blessed memory, Herschel Frankel, for their love and support; my sisters Hedy and Esti; my aunt and uncle Malku and Isser Handler; my nephew David Feiler for his enthusiasm; Jules, my husband, whose love and support still—after nine years of marriage—continue to be a constant surprise and gift; and my special girls Arielle, Shira, and Tehila, who are the musical notes in our family song.

Yitta and Judith would both like to thank an exceptional woman who has given us extraordinary assistance in so many facets of our lives: Anna Ashton. Also, thanks to our beloved friends: Raizy Steg, Pessie Dinnerstein, Bella Friedman, Etta Ansel, Annette Grauman, Ruchama Feuerman, Miriam Kalikstein, and Sarah Laya Landau, for their tremendous support and input all these years. Rabbi Meir Fund remains an invaluable resource and a fount of encyclopedic knowledge whenever we need a nugget of wisdom or Talmudic insight. Many thanks and love to Naomi Mauer and Sheila Abrams of *The Jewish Press* for their wonderful support. We always remember Irene Klass, who started it all, with affection and gratitude. A special note of appreciation to thirteen-year-old intrepid reporter Sruli Steg for unearthing a great story that appears in this book. Thanks, Sruli—you're the best!

There is one particular independent bookstore in Brooklyn—Harnik's—that has championed our work since the very beginning, and we would like to acknowledge their generosity in giving us tremendous support and enthusiasm long before we made "bestseller" status. Their confidence in our material, their excitement, and their happiness for our success, have been profoundly moving and encouraging. To Noreen, Rose, Minnie, and

Evan—we cannot thank you enough for your advocacy and friendship. You guys are the best!

We would also like to thank Eichlers Book Stores, for their friendship and for doing such a fabulous job in showcasing and supporting our most recent book.

On a professional level, we are grateful to our wonderful agent, Richard Pine, and to his associates at the Arthur Pine Agency—Lori Entenman, Sarah Piel, and Catharine Drayton. We have been blessed with a most brilliant and talented editor, Gary M. Krebs, and we are tremendously grateful to be working with such a true professional. His former assistant, Kate Epstein, now promoted to editor, has been an invaluable aid, as is his current assistant, Courtney Nolan. We are thrilled that this sixth volume of *Small Miracles* is once again in the competent hands of a terrific copyeditor—Virginia Rubens—who always makes our prose sing. Also, thanks to Gene Molter, publicist *extraordinaire*, whose dynamism, enthusiasm, and "can do" spirit are refreshing and invigorating; he deserves tremendous gratitude for a wonderful job. And, finally, to visionary publisher Bob Adams, whose initiative and continued championship of *Small Miracles* bless this series—thank you.

Introduction

A young woman and her father have a tender, if tentative, relationship. Warm feelings flow between them, but alas, the feelings have never been fully expressed. The young woman longs for some sign to reassure her that her father's love runs deep, and that a strong bond genuinely connects them.

The two never exchange gifts. The father is a European immigrant who snorts at American commercialism and at gift-giving in general. "Every day should be Father's Day!" he trumpets in scorn, dismissing her modest offerings. "I observe your birth *every* day," he explains cavalierly when he comes home empty-handed on her birthday. Deep in her heart, she knows he loves her, but still she longs for some outward manifestation of the feelings he has locked inside.

One day, during lunch break from her job in Manhattan, the young woman wanders into a bookstore and idly examines the new titles displayed near the front counter. Suddenly, she is struck by one particular book that she knows *instantly* her father—a voracious reader—would love. It's the young woman's first job out of high school and her wages are not high; consequently, she is penny-pinching with uncharacteristic frugality. The hardcover is pricey; its purchase will certainly create a hole in her budget that week. Still, she knows that this particular book will be especially meaningful to her father. For the first time in a long time, she buys him a gift. She knows he never buys one for her, but she won't be petty. She opens her heart and her wallet and makes the purchase.

That night, she waits expectantly for him to return home from a long day's work. She barely waits for him to walk through the door before she gleefully shouts at him: "Guess what! I have a gift for you! I know you're going to love it!" But before she can dart into her room to retrieve the gift-wrapped book, he laughs and tells her with a twinkle in his eye, "Well, guess what? You won't believe it! I have a gift for you, too!"

The young woman is shocked, choked with emotion. Her father has never bestowed a gift upon her before. This is an occasion, a momentous milestone. "Wait!" she says happily. "Let's open our gifts together!"

At the kitchen table—hub of this family's life—the two exchange gift-wrapped packages while the rest of the family looks on. They tear open the packages and then stare at their gifts in shock. In their hands, they both hold copies of the same book!

I know this story well, because it happened to me. The father in the story was mine.

When this incident took place, it was not Father's Day, a national holiday, his wedding anniversary, or anyone's birthday.

Yet on the exact same day, for no apparent reason, we randomly chose to exchange—for the first time in our lives—not only presents, but the *exact same one.* For me, this episode reverberated with special meaning. There was no longer any need to articulate the deep feelings that resided in our souls. The seeming "coincidence" had done all the work for us.

From that day forward, I no longer needed vocal articulation of my father's love. This tender, shining moment, which I will remember all my life, was the full-blown token of his love, and of our deep connection.

Interconnectedness breeds coincidences and miracles. And with whom are we more connected than with the members of our family—our parents, children, siblings, spouses, grandparents, grandchildren, cousins, uncles and aunts? Over the course of the six years in which we have compiled *Small Miracles* stories, Judith and I have been astounded by the tremendous number of "coincidence" stories that testify to the deep and enduring bonds that run among families and create, in their wake, miracles. We have encountered an endless treasure trove of stories recounted by ordinary people that vividly demonstrate the mysterious—even mystical—connections among family members that both change—and save—lives. These bonds transcend time, defy death, and survive through all eternity. Many stories that we have been told (by very credible people indeed) talk of signs and signals that come from beyond this world. One of these incredible stories concerns something that happened to Judith herself.

Several years ago, Judith was dating a young man whom she loved but wasn't sure she wanted to marry. One night, an old friend of her deceased father had a strange dream. In the dream, Judith's father approached him and said: "Listen, my friend. My daughter is going out with a young man whom she can't make up her mind about. I want you to go to her and tell her that I said he is her destined one and she should marry him with no hesitation. She will have a wonderful life with him; I promise."

Judith's father's friend awoke from the dream in a sweat, his heart palpitating. It had seemed so real. He roused his wife in a frenzy and recounted the dream to her. "Should I call Judith and tell her what her father said?" he asked his wife. To which his sensible wife responded, "Superstitious garbage! Don't tell me you really believe her father came to you from beyond the grave?" The father's friend had not been in touch with Judith for many years and had no idea that she was in fact seriously dating someone at the time. So he surrendered to his wife's logic and left the whole thing alone.

Exactly one week later, Judith's father returned to

his old friend in a second dream. "How many times do I have to come to you from the other world?" he berated his old crony. "I told you to go tell my daughter to marry this young man!"

This time her father's friend awoke in fright and decided that—his wife's scorn or not—he was going to do his friend's bidding. Just as he picked up the telephone early the next morning to call Judith and dutifully convey her father's message, she was immersed in prayer. "Please God, send me a sign whether I should marry Jules or not," she begged. Suddenly, the telephone rang. "Hello, Judith?" her father's old friend quavered on the other line. "I don't know how to tell you this, but I have a message for you from your dad . . ."

Judith recently celebrated her ninth wedding anniversary with Jules and they have three wonderful children. Judith needed an extra push—and that's precisely what she got. It just happened to come from an unexpected source!

"Life is not a riddle to be solved," the great author and teacher Joseph Campbell once said, "but a mystery to be experienced." There are things in life—and in this book—that cannot be explained by sheer logic or reason. But love *transcends* both these things.

"Where can you find God?" a great sage once asked. "Wherever you open your heart." And, truly, it is deep within our hearts where our beloved family members reside for all eternity.

The writer Maya Angelou once said: "A bird doesn't sing because it has an answer; it sings because it has a song." This book, then, is our love song to the profound and powerful bonds that inextricably connect family members forever. We may not be able to fully understand or explain away all the enigmas and mysteries contained in some of the stories, but that is not our function. We are here simply to share the Story and sing its Song. May we all be blessed to hear its music, dance to its rhythms, and feel the lightness of being in harmony with humankind, the universe, and God.

Note: Names followed by an asterisk are pseudonyms.

*G*enerally speaking, men's friendships differ from the friendships of women. They are usually more casual and less intense, and they play significantly smaller roles in men's lives than they do in women's. Women depend heavily on their female friends for support, but men frequently favor stoicism and self-reliance over male intimacy to help them weather emotional and professional storms. Of course, this is stereotyping, and there are always the exceptions to the rule. The unusual friendship that developed between Gary Klahr and Steve Barbin was one of them.

When Gary met Steve during a chance encounter in a Connecticut bar some twenty-seven years ago, something clicked. There was an immediate bond, a soul connection. "A guy could have no better friend," Gary wrote on the back of a photograph that he gave to Steve in 1988. "You are truly my brother."

The men were so close that their wives often teased them about their degree and level of attachment. "You guys could have been twins and come out of the same egg," Carolyn Klahr, Gary's wife, used to marvel. "You talk alike. Your voice inflections are alike. You think alike. Sometimes you even finish each other's sentences!"

When Gary's construction worker father, Ben Klahr, died suddenly in 1979 after scaffolding collapsed on him and pinned him underneath, Steve's friendship helped Gary get through the grieving process. Gary was devastated by the death of his father ("the greatest guy I've ever known"), and even though he lay in a coma in the hospital, Gary visited him daily until he died. Gary kept speaking to his father, hoping that somehow his dad could hear his words. The last thing he told him was "Dad, you've worked so hard your whole life to give us all a wonderful life. You were the best father any kid could ever have had. I want you to know that." Recovering from the death of such a beloved and central figure wasn't easy. Steve's friendship helped fill the void that Ben Klahr's death had left in Gary's life.

Gary had three other siblings, but Steve was an only child. Steve had always longed for siblings, and Gary—a couple of years older—assumed the role of mentor and role model.

"We were closer than friends, closer than best friends," Steve said. "Gary became my big brother."

Steve appointed himself curator of Gary's growing collection of professional clippings and mementos, compiling scrapbooks of photographs and press items that bore witness to Gary's two successful careers.

As Gary switched from athletic achievements (which included a brief stint in the National Football League) to acting triumphs (which included Broadway, TV, and parts in movies such as *Married to the Mob, Big, Three Men and a Baby, Legal Eagles,* and *Quick Change*), Steve steadfastly preserved the archives. When Steve married in 1988, there was no question that it would be Gary, his "big brother," whom he would choose to serve as best man.

With Steve married, both friends' lives were now on parallel tracks, heading in the same direction in a seemingly straightforward, uncomplicated way. But on December 30, 1998, Gary received a phone call that changed both men's lives.

"I'm from the Connecticut Department of Children and Families' Office of Foster and Adoption Services," the woman on the other line said. "Is this Gary Klahr?"

The phone call threw Gary off balance and left him momentarily confused. He and his wife Carolyn had three healthy children. They had never spoken about adopting. Had his wife put in an application for adoption and not told him?

"Do you have a chair nearby?" the caseworker asked. "You might want to sit down. I have something to tell you . . . Do you know that you're adopted?"

"It was a bolt out of the blue," Gary remembers. "Like a brick between my eyes, right in the forehead. All my life, for fifty-one years, I had been sure of my identity— that I was the firstborn son of Ben and Marjorie Klahr, blood of their blood, flesh of their flesh. No one—including them—had ever given me any indication to believe otherwise. I never had a premonition. I never had a dream. I had no idea growing up that I was adopted."

The caseworker explained that her phone call had been prompted by a medical search initiated by one of Gary's birth sisters, a woman who had been adopted by another family.

"I've worked on almost four thousand adoption cases so far," the caseworker said, "but I've never encountered a situation like this. You were thirteen siblings, and nine of you were given up for adoption. Twelve of the siblings are still alive."

Gary Klahr had always maintained a strong sense of identity, of knowing exactly who he was and where he was going. Suddenly, in the course of just a few seconds, everything he thought he knew about his life was turned upside down. He had been raised Jewish in the suburbs. His biological parents turned out to be a Roman Catholic couple who lived in a public housing complex. During an eighteen-year marriage, they had had thirteen children, nine of whom they had given away because of dire poverty.

"Are they still alive?" Gary asked.

His biological parents were dead, the caseworker said, but several of his siblings lived nearby.

Gary was numbed by the bombshell that had suddenly been thrown into his lap. The revelations, disclosures, and discoveries were unfolding at a sickening rate, too much to absorb at once. Still, the optimistic spirit inside of him—the part that always looked for a positive spin—prevailed and he said to the social worker: "You know, I have a best friend who's adopted, and he's a great guy. We share a lot of things, and so now we share this!"

"What's your best friend's name?" the caseworker wanted to know.

When Gary told her, she fell silent. "Do you have his phone number?" she asked. "I've been looking for him, too."

"No!" Gary screamed. "You're not saying that . . ."

"Yes, I am," she said. "Steve Barbin is your *brother.*"

That afternoon, Steve Barbin came home from work to hear a message on his answering machine from a woman who said she worked for the state of Connecticut.

Uh, oh, Steve worried, *what did I do wrong? Was there a problem with my tax returns or something?* When he returned the call, the woman asked him, as she had asked Gary previously, "Are you sitting down? I have something to tell you."

Unlike Gary, Steve had always known that he had been adopted. He had felt loved by his adoptive family, and had never speculated about his biological parents. But even if he had, nothing could have prepared Steve for what the caseworker told him next.

"You're one of thirteen siblings," she said.

"Wow!" he exclaimed.

"There's something else I have to tell you," she said.

Something else? he thought. *What more could there possibly be?*

"Is there anybody in your life," she asked, "about

whom people have said 'you're so much alike you could be brothers'?"

Steve didn't hesitate.

"Are you telling me," he demanded, "that Gary Klahr is my *blood brother*?"

"Yes, I am," she said.

"Gar?" Steve called his best friend after he had had a long discussion with the case worker. "Do you believe this?"

"Steve," Gary said. "We've always lived our lives as if we were brothers anyway. Nothing's changed; it's only confirmed. This just makes our relationship more special than it was before."

Over the next few months, Gary and Steve were gradually reunited with four other siblings, and ultimately they fostered close and substantial ties with one another. And in the course of those meetings, there were more surprises to come: One of the siblings turned out to be Richard, Gary's workout partner for the last fifteen years; another one was Micka, a woman Gary had briefly dated in 1979.

Gary shudders when he contemplates the worst-case scenario that might have occurred with Micka. "That coincidence is a true cautionary tale about the risks of private adoptions and sealed records," he says.

"But the story I share with Steve is different. That's a story of love, friendship, and ultimately brotherhood. As strange and tangled as our story may seem, my siblings and I choose to say that this is a wonderful story of how we have come back together again." ❀

*I*n the dark of night, combat-weary soldiers often find a reprieve from the day's wages of war: the unremitting gunfire; the haunting cries of the wounded; the close and constant skirmishes with death. The battlefields drenched in the blood of the dying are obscured by the inky blackness of nightfall, and troops enjoy the temporary respite to smoke a cigarette, murmur softly to one another, or simply contemplate the moonlit sky.

But on this particular night—a night in 1862 when the Civil War was raging—the moon was shrouded by thick clouds, and there was no respite for Union army captain Robert Ellicombe. He was encamped with his men near Harrison's Landing in Virginia, and the Confederate army was on the other side of the narrow strip of land, far too close for comfort or security. Fierce gun battles had been raging all day, and although the Confederate army had sustained far greater losses than the Union side, Captain Ellicombe tasted neither victory nor triumph. In this war, brother fought brother, and entire families were torn apart by the strife. The human toll that this war exacted sickened him. A good man, he railed against the unnecessary and senseless loss of life, even while he faithfully executed his superiors' orders.

Captain Ellicombe was standing outside his tent, immersed in his thoughts, reviewing the day's events and preparing tomorrow's strategies, when a sound pierced his intense concentration. It was the low and anguished moaning of a soldier—a soldier clearly wounded and somehow forgotten on the battlefield nearby. *Was it a Union soldier or a member of the Confederate army?* Captain Ellicombe wondered. *The universal cries of suffering know no distinctions*, he thought. His glance swept the camp to see whether anyone else had registered the unmistakable sound, but aside from the few sentries who could not leave their posts, no one seemed astir. There did not seem to be any men around whom he could quickly dispatch to the soldier's side, and the soldier might well need help . . . fast. *But what if it isn't a Union soldier; what if it's a Confederate man instead?* he asked himself. *Even a Confederate soldier shouldn't have to be in such pain. Even the enemy deserves medical attention.* Ellicombe knew he was risking his life, and perhaps for the wrong man, too, but only one overriding thought dominated now: *I have to help.*

Crawling on his stomach to avoid stray bullets, Captain Ellicombe inched his way toward the stricken man. Now he was grateful for the moonless night, for it offered him cover and concealed his movements from the enemy. His only guide to the wounded soldier was the faint groaning the soldier emitted, but the groans were fading ominously even as Ellicombe slowly advanced. When he reached the soldier, Ellicombe could sense that he was barely alive; but he refused to give up on him. He pulled him back to his camp, and only when he reached the safety of his own lines did he feel for the man's pulse. It was gone. He had been too late. The anonymous soldier for whom he had risked his life was dead.

Ellicombe lit a lantern and saw for the first time that the soldier was wearing a Confederate uniform. Then he shone the lantern in the young man's face and froze. He knew the distinguishing features, the familiar contours of that face well. They belonged to his own son.

His son, a talented and brilliant composer, had been studying music at a well-known academy in the South when the Civil War broke out. Without telling his father, he had enlisted in the Confederate army. It was exceedingly difficult—if not impossible—for families caught on different sides to communicate with one another during this time. Captain Ellicombe had not heard from his son for a very long time, but had prayed that he was safe. As the months passed with no word from him, he had become increasingly tormented about his welfare—plagued by doubts, riddled with fear. *Where was he?* Now he knew with certitude exactly where his son could be found. Captain Ellicombe cradled him in his arms and wept, a broken man.

Later, after he had exhausted the seemingly endless well of tears, Captain Ellicombe thought of searching his son's pockets. Perhaps they would yield certain clues to the last few months of his son's life—the period in which he no longer knew him. Wild with grief to know his son through his possessions and personal mementos, Captain Ellicombe hunted through his son's clothes for hints, traces, signs—suggestions of what kind of man he had been and why he had joined the Confederate army. But other than standard ID, not much of significance was found, except for some musical notes scribbled on a piece of paper—apparently an original musical composition by his talented son, and perhaps his only one.

The next morning, Captain Ellicombe requested permission to give his son a full military burial. His superiors felt tremendous compassion for their grieving comrade—a man who had pulled his own son from the trenches of the dead—and gave their partial consent. Even though the boy was a member of the enemy camp, an adversary, a traitor, he was also Ellicombe's beloved child. How could they deny a father's poignant farewell? But since the boy had been a Confederate soldier, they refused Ellicombe's petition for a full military band to play a funeral dirge for his son. We will give you one musician, they said. You can choose which one.

In his hand, Captain Ellicombe clutched the piece of paper he had found in his son's pocket, the paper on which his son's original musical composition was scribbled. His last will and testament. His legacy. Captain Ellicombe was not as musically gifted as his son, but his father's intuition was strong. He chose a bugler and asked him to play his son's melody as a final tribute.

Captain Ellicombe's yearning to commemorate his son's brief life was fulfilled far beyond the measure of his expectations. He assumed the melody would be played once — and then be forgotten. How could he have known, on that fateful night, that when he pulled the crumpled sheet of music from his son's bloodstained jacket, a beloved melody would be born and would endure through the generations?

Over the years, the son's unforgettable composition would become a musical legacy to America. The haunting and familiar music has now become integral to military funerals, wreath-laying and memorial services, and as a tattoo each evening at military facilities as a call to close a soldier's day. It is a melody inexorably woven into our country's history and traditions — the beloved music known to us all as "Taps." ❀

y father is a sentimental person. He may not like to admit it, but he is. To him, it is often the *meaning* behind something that is important, rather than its pure financial worth. A perfect example of where his priorities lie was demonstrated by an incident that occurred several years ago.

My grandmother passed away in December 1992. She had lived in a mobile home in a small town in Florida, and like a lot of people, had collected a tremendous amount of "junk" throughout the years. It wasn't junk to her, but to others it surely seemed that way. My father flew in from California to attend the funeral, and my uncle drove down from Georgia. Almost immediately afterwards, my uncle and his wife started going through my grandmother's things and throwing them away. Each night, after everyone had left, my father (who was staying in my grandmother's mobile home) would go through those bags of "junk" just to make sure there wasn't something he wanted to keep. In one of those bags my father found a simple three-tiered wire basket that had always hung in her kitchen and that held fruits and vegetables. At most, it was probably worth a couple of bucks, but for some reason it reminded my father of my grandmother. So he pulled it out of the trash and took it back to California with him.

The one thing of modest value that everyone noticed was missing was her wedding ring set. As long as I can remember, she never took her rings off—but when she died, they were not on her fingers. Before the funeral, everyone in the family hunted frantically for them, because we knew she would want to be buried wearing them. We searched everywhere in the mobile home but turned up nothing. It was really very strange. No one could figure out what she might have done with them, and we were sure that none of her friends had taken them. The rings weren't worth all that much money; it was what they stood for that made them valuable.

Well, the mystery was not solved, and everyone went back home. A few weeks after my father got back home, he called to tell me that the rings had been found. Shocked, I asked him where on earth they had been. He told me that one morning, while drinking coffee, he was looking at the wire basket he had pulled out of the trash and noticed that there was something stuck to it. He got up to look—and there they were, safety-pinned to the basket!

It's funny, but after he told me, I could just picture my grandmother doing that. I'm sure she thought nothing would happen to them there—and as it turned out, she was right.

To this day, the basket hangs in my father's kitchen.

—NICOLE MOHRMAN

I am not really sure when my story begins. Perhaps my odyssey starts with the arrival of an old photograph of my great-great-grandparents, Mr. and Mrs. Yitzchok Klein from Miskole, Hungary, circa 1860s. They were the parents of my mother's grandmother, Katherine (Golda) Glasser. Apparently, the photo had been distributed at a Glasser family reunion that had taken place while I was out of the country. Those who didn't attend received the photo in the mail instead.

The timing of its arrival was somewhat meaningful for me, because I had just returned home from a two-year stay in Israel, where I had attended a Jewish school in Jerusalem and had searched for my roots. My quest for answers led me to a deeper understanding of my faith, and as a result, I took the plunge and changed from a lobster-eating California free spirit to a kosher, Sabbath-observing freer spirit.

The photo, which arrived at about that time, looked like 100 others from that era: a solemn couple standing against a wallpapered backdrop, he in a three-quarter coat, sporting a handlebar mustache, and a long, curved pipe; she in a long-sleeved, floor-length dress with something that looked suspiciously like an apron around her waist. What caught my eye, however, was that her hair was concealed beneath a beaded head covering—the unmistakable sign of an observant Jew. I yearned to know more, so when another Glasser family reunion was scheduled to take place at the Skokie Hilton in Chicago, I jumped at the opportunity.

At the reunion, to my disappointment, I learned little else about my great-great-grandparents. But when I asked the cousins if they knew where my great-grandparents, the Glassers, were buried, one of them produced an old caretaker's receipt from Waldheim Jewish Cemetery—right there in Chicago—with the plot and section number of my great-grandfather, Joseph.

The reunion ended on Sunday and I was scheduled to fly back to New York that evening. Then Rabbi and Mrs. Lasovsky, the couple who had hosted me during my stay, made me an offer I couldn't resist. If I were willing to change my flight, Rabbi Lasovsky would take me to Waldheim Cemetery on his way to work Monday morning and help me locate Joseph's grave. Rescheduling my flight turned out to be impossible, so, to my own astonishment, I forfeited my ticket.

Early the next morning, I stood in the caretaker's office at Waldheim Cemetery with Rabbi Lasovsky and the precious receipt. As it turned out, Joseph was buried in a family plot with a host of other relatives, and Katherine, my great-grandmother, was buried in a different section. I felt I had hit paydirt—literally.

Armed with a map, we began to look for Katherine first. After thirty minutes of fruitless searching, we made a frustrated cell phone call to the caretaker. He offered to come out to help us, and another ten minutes passed. When he arrived, he directed us to her grave and we saw that, oddly, we had practically been standing right next to it.

As I stood by the grave, I experienced a strange sort of intimacy. She had given me life, yet I had never known her. I knew she would have loved me and I felt the loss. I cringed at the thought of her painful death at forty-four from a simple appendectomy, and of the grief of the eleven children she left behind—one of them my grandmother.

We had been at the cemetery for more than an hour, so I rushed through my prayers. Rabbi Lasovsky also said a prayer on my great-grandmother's behalf and, kind man that he is, offered to help me find my great-grandfather's grave—even though he was now going to be late for work.

It was as easy to find Joseph as it had been hard to find Katherine. He lay in the family plot, clearly the patriarch in a world of past Glassers. The scene was so compelling that it was impossible not to be drawn into the story told by the graves. Rising from the middle of the grove was Joseph's headstone engraved entirely in Hebrew lettering. It was clear, the Rabbi explained, that the people who had buried Joseph had understood the tradition and had known what they were doing. But with his death it seemed that the connection to the Jewish way of life in the Glasser family had died, too. Scattered around him were headstones that were barely identifiable as Jewish. There were almost no Hebrew names, and errors had been made in the few Hebrew words that had been used.

Rabbi Lasovsky and I chatted for a while and then he quietly said a *Kel Rachamman*—a prayer for the dead, his words thudding into the thick stillness that lingers in graveyards. We had long since forgotten about the time.

Suddenly, as we stood lost in thought, we were startled by the sound of leaves crunching. It slowly began to dawn on me that people were approaching. But we were nowhere near a footpath where people would ordinarily tread—and we were standing in a family plot. *Who are these people?* I wondered.

As the sound drew nearer, a disembodied voice rang out. "Here they are," it said. Abruptly, an older man appeared and pointed to the graves in front of us. A woman and a younger man trailed behind him.

Not knowing the correct etiquette for meeting people in graveyards, I hesitated. Should I say something like, "Who are you here to see?" I decided that didn't seem appropriate so instead I asked, "Are you here for these graves?" When I received a "yes," I managed to stammer the words, "Who are you?" Silence. I tried again. "Who are you?" The only people in that cemetery more flabbergasted than Rabbi Lasovsky and I were our three visitors.

I realized that I had better start explaining if we were going to get anywhere, so I began recounting my family history. "My name is Jeannie Silver. My mother, Jacquelyn, is the daughter of William Rice and Jennie Glasser. Her grandmother was Katherine Glasser and her grandfather was Joseph and this is his grave," I said, pointing to his headstone. "My great-grandfather."

"And *my grandfather*," the woman responded.

Unbelievably, standing before me was my mother's first cousin, Gloria. She and her husband had flown from their home in Las Vegas to Chicago to attend the funeral of his mother—which had been going on at Waldheim Cemetery while the Rabbi and I were searching for Katherine's grave. The service had just finished and they had decided to pay their respects to Gloria's parents and her brother, Sherwin, who had died at age four. The young man accompanying them was my cousin Howard, one of Gloria's three sons.

It was magical. It was serendipitous. It was a moment that hit Rabbi Lasovsky and me like a freight train and we couldn't help but feel that we had been brushed by the divine.

I was so excited that I became hyperactive. "I live in New York," I babbled, "but I came to Chicago for a family reunion." I ran to the car and returned with a book from the reunion that contained addresses and diagrams of the various Glasser family trees. Gloria's tree had appeared, but she had not been invited. The entry in the address section explained why. It read: "Gloria Brown—address unknown."

I stood at the gravesite and finished filling in the rest of Gloria's tree, all the while trying to grasp the significance of this remarkable meeting. I felt that there must be something important that should be said or done, but I couldn't figure out what it was. I was clinging to each moment in an attempt to make it last, although deep inside I knew it was impossible. And then, as hard as I tried to make time stand still, everyone needed to be on his way.

Before we separated, Gloria asked me about the reunion. "Where was it?"

"It was in the Skokie Hilton—it ended yesterday," I replied.

"I was in the Skokie Hilton yesterday!" she screamed. So were about twenty of her relatives—but she never knew or met them.

Gloria asked me who had been at the reunion, but I had been too overwhelmed to remember. Later that evening, I was desperate to share my story with someone, and I thought of Jack Rassof, the cousin who had given me the receipt that had led me to Waldheim Cemetery.

"You'll never believe what happened today," I said,

and began to relate the day's events. "I met Gloria Glasser in the cemetery."

"Gloria Glasser?" Jack asked excitedly. "I've been looking for her for *years!* I lost track of her when she moved from Chicago," he said.

"Well, now she's on her way to her son in Ohio," I told him, and gave him the number that she had given me at our grandfather's gravesite.

I am still in touch with Gloria and so is Jack. I have now met two of her sons and have conversed with a third. We have exchanged more family historical information, and about a half-dozen cousins have been reconnected as a result of our meeting.

As for me, I never envisioned that a simple pilgrimage to an ancestor's grave would resurrect a lost family, and breathe new life into faltering family ties. ✿

—JEANNIE SILVER

*S*usie was only sixteen years old when Lillian Vaccaro, the woman behind the grocery store counter, began paying special attention to her.

Taking the same route home from school every afternoon, Susie often darted into the local "mom and pop" grocery store that she passed to pick up supplies for her mother. There was always something her mother needed or was running out of—milk, eggs, juice—and, since her mother worked all day and didn't get home until six, Susie was happy to run small errands for her.

Both Susie and the grocery store seemed to be relics of a different age. Susie was an old-fashioned type of girl who studied diligently, helped her mother with housework, and volunteered at a hospital over weekends. Lillian's Pick N' Pay, the store where she shopped, was also a throwback to a bygone era. It was musty, cramped, and out-of-date, but friendliness and cheer were always on hand. Susie preferred the warmth of the small shop to the antiseptic atmosphere of larger supermarkets.

Over the years, Lillian had become quite fond of

Susie. Whenever she dropped in, the young girl was always kind and polite. From her observation tower at the counter, the eagle-eyed, gray-haired Italian grandmother often watched Susie open doors for incoming and outgoing customers, help older women struggling with packages, and retrieve and return change that other people dropped. "You know," she said one day to Susie out of the blue, "you would be perfect for my grandson!"

Susie blushed a deep red and then laughed. "Hey," she protested, "I'm only sixteen! I don't even date!"

Mrs. Vaccaro's disappointment showed. "You're only sixteen," she echoed in disbelief. "Who would believe it? You're *soooo* mature!"

"Everyone tells me that," Susie acknowledged. "Maybe it's because my dad died when we were young and I help my mother a lot. But yes, I'm only sixteen and my mother doesn't allow me to go out yet. But thanks anyway!"

Susie, ever sensitive, wanted to make sure Mrs. Vaccaro didn't feel rejected in any way. She was, after all, the young man's grandma. So, as she left the store, Susie called over her shoulder: "Can I take a rain check? How about we discuss your grandson—if he's still available—two years from now?"

"It's a deal!" Mrs. Vaccaro smiled. "As I said, I think you'd be perfect for each other!"

Afterwards, Susie would often wonder what Mrs. Vaccaro had meant when she exclaimed, "It's a deal!"

because it didn't seem likely that she (or her grandson) would wait two years. Yet every time Susie came in through the door, Lillian would kid her and say, "Hurry and grow up, I have my grandson on hold for you!"

Inwardly, Susie would groan about the comments and consider shopping at the brand-new supermarket instead. But too many others had defected there, leaving the Vaccaros with less and less income—and Susie didn't have the heart to do it to them.

Finally Susie snapped. "Mrs. Vaccaro! I promise I'll date your grandson . . . but you have to leave me alone until I'm ready!"

But when Susie was finally allowed to date, Lillian was no longer around to set her up. Slowed down by age, the Vaccaros decided to close the store and relocate to a retirement community in Arizona. The property on which the store stood was sold to a real estate developer. In Arizona, the elderly woman succumbed to a fatal stroke, and her husband died a few years later of a heart attack. Soon, the cozy little shop on the corner was gone, replaced by yet another gleaming, sterile supermarket.

Susie would have been outraged by the change, but she was no longer home to see the property's transformation. She was thousands of miles away in graduate school, where her life had turned exciting. Beyond the stimulation of her studies and ambitions for a career, she had met a young man named Chris who seemed to be her soul mate. They dated for several months, and during spring break, Susie brought him home. Her mother, siblings, and friends approved wholeheartedly. *I knew they would,* Susie thought. *We are so much alike. It's as if we were cut from the same cloth.*

One evening during the visit home, Susie and Chris were taking a long walk when they passed the gleaming new supermarket that had been erected on the site of the old Pick N' Pay. "Yecch!" Susie groaned, as she surveyed through the large, shiny windows the neatly stacked shelves, the immaculately swept floors, the rows of electronic checkout counters, the unforgiving fluorescent lights. "I hate these . . . what do you call them . . . these behemoths!"

"I love loving an English major!" Chris punched her playfully on the shoulder. "What is a behemoth?"

"You know, these giants! These corporations! These companies that swallow up the little people and replace the personal touch with coupons!"

"I know what you mean," Chris sighed. "The little mom and pop stores are practically a thing of the past. They barely exist anymore, certainly not in the big cities. Some small towns still have them, I guess. But hey, you know, it's the times we're living in—it's called 'the malling of America.'"

"Actually," he continued, "my grandparents used to run that kind of store. Did I ever tell you that they used to live in this city?"

"You're kidding!" Susie shouted. "How come you never told me that before?"

"Well, after my grandmother died, my grandfather moved to Arizona for several years before he passed on, so I guess I kinda think 'Arizona' when I think of my grandfather's last home. But yes, they did live in this city and they ran a small store. I think they called it Pick N' Pay or something like that."

"Wait a second." Susie trembled with excitement. "Your grandmother's first name wasn't *Lillian,* was it?"

"Why, yes." Now it was Chris's turn to look at *her* in astonishment. "Now how would you ever know that?"

"Because Lillian's Pick N' Pay was located right here on the corner, where the supermarket is, and I used to shop there all the time!"

"You're kidding!" Chris gasped.

"I used to talk with your grandmother all the time."

"You're kidding!" Chris repeated dumbly.

"But wait a second . . . your last name isn't Vaccaro?"

"They were my grandparents from my *mother's* side. Vaccaro is my mother's maiden name."

They were both silent for a moment as they absorbed the impact of the synchronicity. But there was more to come.

"Hey, Chris," Susie asked, suddenly recalling a long-forgotten conversation. "How many grandchildren did your grandmother have?"

"Between my mother and her two sisters, seven in all."

"How many grand*sons?*"

"Oh, just me. Girls seem to run in my mother's family. I was the only grandson."

"Well, if you're the only grandson, Chris, then I have something important to tell you . . ."

Weeks later, when they got engaged, Susie traveled to California to meet Chris's family, but along the way they made a short stopover. To Arizona. Where the two made a pilgrimage to a cemetery and paid homage to a wise Italian grandmother.

"Thank you, Mrs. Vaccaro," Susie whispered at the gravesite. "I don't know exactly how you did it, but one thing is for sure . . . you can never argue with an Italian grandmother!" ✿

*D*avid Beard is sure that the bizarre cluster of birthdays in his family has got to mean *something,* but darn if he knows what it is.

He first realized that something strange was afoot when his daughter Emily was born on the 12th day of the 12th month at 12 minutes past 12 (December 12th at 12:12 P.M.). Such a coincidence could not go unnoticed, even by the most oblivious members of the human species. Under ordinary circumstances, the bizarre numerical confluence of both time and date would have elicited a chuckle — or, at the very least, a smile — from David, had it not suddenly struck him: *He* had been born on none other than the 4th day of the 4th month at 4:40 P.M., and his wife Helen had come into the world on the 10th day of the 10th month at . . . you guessed it . . . 10:10 P.M.

That would have been weird enough, but the coincidences didn't stop there. The Beards' older son Harry made his debut as a newborn on the 6th of the 6th

(June 6th) at 6:06, while the matriarch of the family, grandmother Sylvia (who apparently initiated the whole cycle) was born on 11/11 at . . . 11:11. This most recent Beard birth has left David scratching his head in perplexity. There definitely has to be some kind of design here, he opines, but Lord knows if he can figure it out.

Bookmakers in London (near where the births took place) told reporters that the odds of such a phenomenon occurring are about a million to one. They said, however, that if any member of the Beard family ever wanted to place bets with *them* on *anything*, they'd definitely consider narrower odds.

The strange sequence of events that culminated in Emily's birth proved that you just can't push nature . . . or fate. Emily's birth by Caesarean section had been scheduled in advance by Mrs. Beard's doctor for 10 A.M. the morning of December 12th. Things didn't go as planned, however. Various medical complications ensued, including the distressing inability of the nurses to get a needle into Mrs. Beard's arm and hook her up to the IV drip. Because of all the delays, it was past noon when Emily arrived at St. Mary's Hospital in Portsmouth.

The doctor looked up at the wall clock and instructed the nurses to record the time of birth: ". . . Little girl, born at . . ." He paused for a second, and everyone in the delivery room, including the proud parents, raised their eyes together. "It was exactly

12 minutes past 12," said Mr. Beard. "We kind of just looked at each other after that."

"It's weird," he ventured.

The Beards don't plan to have any more children, but they do intend to start playing the lottery. And you don't have to be a brain surgeon to predict which numbers they'll use. ❀

*I*n crowded cities, cramped apartments, packed movie theaters, and malls teeming with shoppers, Americans these days cry out for space. So it's no surprise that, after exchanging cursory "hellos" and brief nods, most airplane passengers settle into their seats, pull out a newspaper or a headset, and studiously ignore their seatmate. The last thing they want to contend with is the prospect of a garrulous neighbor who will intrude upon their privacy. They need their solitude and are prepared to go to great lengths to protect it.

But sometimes, marvelous opportunities — for a professional contact, a new friend, or a fresh romance — are forfeited when barriers are erected. When we emit the unspoken body language that signals "Leave me alone," we may have gained our solitude but lost something in turn. And, in rare cases, it may even be something as important as a human life.

Thankfully, Allen Van Meter, a warm, genial man of forty-three who makes friends easily, was not the type to sit in his seat oblivious to the stranger next to him. Instead of averting his eyes politely or staring blankly ahead, he amiably looked over his seatmate's shoulder and gazed curiously at the sheet of paper she was studying. He tapped her politely on the arm and asked, "Hope you don't mind my asking, but what in the world is that?"

Janet Larson, the forty-eight-year-old stranger seated next to him, explained that the drawing in her lap was a diagram of a kidney. Janet explained that she was on her way to Louisiana via Memphis to donate a kidney in a desperate attempt to save her dying sister, Deborah White. Deborah had originally been suffering from liver disease, and had had a liver transplant in 1997. Her body had begun almost immediately to reject the transplanted liver, and she had been given antirejection drugs. These, in turn, were now destroying Deborah's kidneys. Janet's kidney donation was only a half-measure that would buy time for her sister but not save her. What was really needed to save Deborah's life was another liver, and if she didn't get one soon, she would die. "Deborah's been on a waiting list for a new liver for over six months," Janet told Allen, "but there's a tremendous shortage of cadaver organs, as I'm sure you know. The doctor says she's sitting on a time bomb."

Allen looked at Janet Larson thoughtfully as she recounted her sister's woes. He, too, had grabbed the early morning flight out of Jacksonville because of a family crisis, but it was of an entirely different kind. The night before, Allen's nephew, twenty-five-year-old Michael

Gibson, had been horsing around with a gun he thought wasn't loaded, and had accidentally shot himself. He had been declared brain dead, and Allen had gotten the call at midnight and had grabbed the first flight out that morning to comfort his sister in Springfield, Illinois. Allen knew that the family had decided to donate Michael's organs.

Allen sat silently in his seat for a few minutes, stunned by the coincidence that had placed him next to Janet. *Her* sister needed a liver, and *his* nephew's family was about to donate one. After a short pause, he tapped her on the shoulder again. "We need to do something about this," he said.

Janet was dubious about the proposal, but he insisted that they try, and she finally relented. Using a phone on the airplane, Janet called the hospital where her sister was confined and asked the nurse in charge whether a "direct donation" (in which donors or their families designate a particular person to receive an organ) could be made. The nurse said yes. Then Allen got on the phone with the hospital in Springfield and told the nurse what they wanted to do. "It's impossible," the nurse answered. "We've already wheeled your nephew into the operating room to remove him from life support and begin harvesting his organs. You're too late."

"This is *not* impossible," Allen said urgently. "Anything and everything is possible. We weren't seated next to each other for nothing. This is coming from God. Can you stop the procedure?"

Impressed by his words, the nurse promised she would try. She was able to reach the doctors before they started their work.

Janet called her sister with the incredible news. "Please don't get too excited," she said, "but I think I may have found you a liver."

Between them, Janet and Allen made $80 worth of phone calls from the plane. Soon, all the passengers were drawn into the unfolding drama, and ordinary conversation came to a halt.

Meanwhile, the staffs of the two hospitals—the one where Michael Gibson's body lay on life support and the one where Deborah White lay dying—were caught up in an emotional roller coaster of their own. Phone calls and faxes flew back and forth as they feverishly worked to ascertain whether Michael and Deborah's blood and tissue types matched. When it was determined that they did, the hospitals arranged for the organ to be transported and transplanted. The New Orleans Memorial Hospital chartered a private plan to fly the organ down.

Deborah White was wheeled into surgery at 11:30 that night. It was only then that doctors discovered that the main artery to her liver was almost completely blocked. They had not been aware of the problem, and subsequently said that she could have died at any time. Deborah could have succumbed in a matter of days—or even hours. The liver had come just in the nick of time.

When Allen Van Meter had grabbed the first plane

out of Jacksonville to rush to his sister's side, he was accompanied by his wife, who planned to fly with him. But he had been told there was only one seat left in the entire plane and that only one of them could go.

Allen had been distressed that his wife had to be left behind, and he was also unhappy with the seat's location—all the way in the back of the plane. "Don't you have any other seat?" he had originally asked. "It's our very last one, sir," the clerk replied. "You want it or not?"

How could Allen or his wife have known he was bound for a date with destiny? ✿

*T*he first time I met Rose, I was standing in six inches of snow at an uncovered bus stop; there weren't any benches. My car was in the body shop being repaired, and taking the bus was a new experience for me. The wind was blowing, and it was so cold I needed to keep stamping my feet so they wouldn't get numb. In the depth of my misery, I almost didn't see her approaching, struggling against the wind as she fought to keep her balance on the icy sidewalk.

When she stopped not too far away, she greeted me politely and asked if I was going to work. I nodded, suddenly wary. *Was she going to ask me for money?* I wondered. Then she told me she was on her way to work, too, but that she'd rather be home in a nice warm bed. I agreed, and then glanced away, hoping to avoid further conversation; I didn't want to talk to this strange person who'd casually invaded my life.

I didn't want to look at her, either; she was less prepared for the cold than I was. While she was wearing two scarves and a pair of earmuffs, there were holes in her sweatpants, her tennis shoes were badly worn, and her coat was threadbare.

Still trying to ignore her by pretending to watch for the bus, I felt a hand on my arm. It was a frail touch.

"Sir?" The voice was frail, too. "Sir?" she repeated.

I turned my attention to her and looked down. She was holding a pair of gloves out to me.

"Why don't you put these on? You look terribly cold," she said in a voice that reminded me of my ninth-grade English teacher.

Embarrassed, I politely declined, telling her I had a high tolerance for cold. Again, I deliberately looked away.

"I'd be honored if you would," she said against the wind, her hand on my arm again. "They're my son's, and he doesn't need them."

Again, I said no, adding that I might lose them, and that her son might need them later. I didn't let it show in my voice, but I was growing annoyed. Why wouldn't this woman just leave me alone?

She insisted once more, pointing out that one of my hands was bleeding. The skin across my knuckles had split from the cold; she must have noticed it when I was smoking.

I refused once more, though this time somewhat more forcefully—yet still polite. I reminded her that the bus would be here soon, and I wouldn't need them then. Until then, my pockets would do just fine. I looked away once more, facing in the direction the bus would come from.

"I really wish you would," she tried the fourth time. I was starting to feel trapped. My mother had taught me to be courteous and now I was feeling pressure to accept the gloves. But my pride wouldn't let me, and my mother wasn't there. I was about to refuse again when I saw the bus at the top of the hill. I felt sudden relief.

"Oh, look," I pointed out as casually as I could. "Here's the bus."

"I'm so glad," she responded softly. "Now remember, when you get to work, wash your hands very carefully. Don't use hot water; lukewarm is best. And if you have medicated soap, use it; it will help prevent infection." Then she opened her purse and clumsily pulled out a small bottle of hand cream. She pressed it into my hand—the one that was already out with my transfer ticket—before I could stop her. "Then put this on."

I mumbled a "thanks" just as the bus pulled up. I let her board first, partly out of courtesy, but primarily so I could see where she sat. I waited impatiently as she struggled up the steep steps. She cheerfully greeted the driver by name and asked him how he was before showing her bus pass and sitting down. I boarded quickly, gave the driver my transfer ticket, and picked the seat furthest away from her. I pulled out a paperback and buried my nose in it, shutting Rose and everyone else out of my world.

Her stop was before mine, but I didn't notice; I was too busy ignoring Rose and everyone else.

The next morning, thankfully, was warmer. Most of the snow had melted, the warm breeze was refreshing, and the sky was clear and blue. I felt good, and for a change, I didn't dread the fifteen-minute wait for my connection. Suddenly, I saw her. She was about a block away, her head slightly lowered, her back bent a little. I got the impression it hurt her to walk. But there was a bright smile on her face as our eyes met, and she gave me a little wave.

Despite her slow pace, it wasn't long before she was standing beside me.

"Good morning!" she greeted me.

"Good morning," I answered back, putting a half-hearted smile on my face.

"I'm sorry," she abruptly announced.

"Excuse me?" *Why was she apologizing to me? Did she think she had been rude yesterday morning by offering me her son's gloves?* That's when I noticed hers; two fingertips stuck out of the right one.

"I was impolite yesterday for speaking to you without introducing myself. I'm Rose." She removed a glove, the one with the two holes at the fingertips, and offered the frail hand—thin and lightly lined with pale blue veins on the back. I gently shook it.

"I'm Pete." I released her hand with difficulty; she didn't seem to want to let go.

"Pete," she repeated, with another smile. Some of the wrinkles disappeared, and her eyes became wide and bright; I felt I could see deep into her soul. "That's my son's name, too."

"What a coincidence," I stammered. *Oh, no. Now what?* I thought. I was back on the defensive again, struggling to look away.

Rose suddenly changed the subject. "It's such a beautiful morning!" She took a deep, asthmatic breath, capturing freshness and clutching it to her. I agreed that it was, but she went on speaking.

"It reminds me of when I was a little girl," she continued, taking another wheezing deep breath. Inside, I groaned. *Didn't Rose sense that I just wanted to be left alone?*

"The mornings were always beautiful then. I remember helping my mother with the laundry; it was the first thing we did after breakfast. Mom said that since we had to hang the clothes out to dry we had to use all the sunlight God gave us. When I was older, I decided she just liked mornings."

Politeness made me look away from the street and back at Rose. Her eyes were alive, animated by the past, and the wrinkles weren't quite so obvious.

"I can still hear the wooden clothespins; the springs always squeaked when I opened them. I can even hear the creaks of the laundry basket when Mother moved it. It was woven wicker, not the plastic we have today."

Oh, no, I was thinking. *I'm alone with a crazy woman who has Alzheimer's or something. Why me?* I just want to get on the bus and get to work.

"I used to worry about the clothes getting dirty if the wind blew too hard. There wasn't any grass under the clothesline, you see, and the clothes might get dirty. One morning I asked Father to move the clothesline for us. His name was Pete, too. I named my only son after him." A sad little look vanished into another smile.

"He just laughed," Rose continued. "He teased me that if my feet weren't so big the grass would still be there, and what was I trying to do, kill more grass? I laughed with him, and then he hugged me. He always hugged me when we laughed."

She fell silent again. Her eyes were soft and glassy; *was she on some kind of medication, too?* I wondered.

"He gave the best hugs in the world."

I heard it before I saw it—the sound of salvation in the form of a downshifting diesel engine and squeaky brakes. Rescue was at hand.

Again, I allowed her to board first, and the same scenario played out: she was slow to get up the stairs; she made small talk with the driver; and she went to the same seat. I too went to the same seat as the day before and immersed myself in my book.

The next day was worse than the first two. Rose picked up where she had left off the day before. "I was his only daughter, you see. He spent every spare minute he had with me. We even used to go on our own picnics. I'll never forget them, but there was one . . ." Her voice trailed off, and that dreamy look was back in her blue eyes.

Then she continued: "It was a morning just like this one, clear and sunny with the most beautiful clouds in a perfect sky. It was my sixth birthday, and Father and I were going to have a picnic breakfast. I was so excited! I remember being the first one up. I tiptoed out to the kitchen and made peanut butter and jelly sandwiches. When I got out the waxed paper to wrap them, I almost dropped the box." Rose smiled at the memory, but I could tell she was remembering a lot more than she was telling.

"Then I picked out two apples and polished them with the sleeve of my nightgown. I spent the most time on his, and I even tried to pull the stem out but it broke off, so I had to polish the other apple even better. This time I left the stem alone. Then I went out to the shed and got the picnic basket. The napkins were still inside from our last picnic. They were the big red-checked ones, the kind Father liked. He used to say they had to be big to fit over his belly." Her smile faded to sad, then back to normal.

"I shook them out and then I folded them up again." Her gloved hands twitched a little, moving slowly up and down, then back and forth; she must have worked hard on those napkins, especially her father's.

"I took the basket inside. It was so big; I had to use two hands. After I packed it, I tiptoed back to my room and got dressed. Then I went to Mother and Father's room. They were still sleeping, Mother on her side, and Father on his back. I went around the bed. I tapped on Father's chest, but he didn't wake up." Rose paused a moment for a deep breath, as if talking was using up more air than she could take in. Her eyes weren't as bright now. She took a second wheezing breath.

After the third wheeze, she continued: "I tapped again, and I kissed him on the cheek, but he still didn't wake up. Then I whispered in his ear. I hoped he wouldn't wake up laughing, because I didn't want Mother to wake up." She hesitated again, and I started to get an inkling of what was next.

"I whispered in his ear again, but he still wouldn't wake up. I got scared and stopped whispering. That's when Mom woke up. When she couldn't wake Father, she sent me out of the room. She was crying. So was I."

The bus glided to a stop in front of us, surprising me. I hadn't heard its diesel engine labor up the hill.

She laboriously started up the steps, then stopped and looked at me. "I don't eat peanut butter and jelly anymore."

When I took my usual seat, I left my book where it was; this time I wanted to see where she got off. When she pulled the cord to signal the stop, I looked around. The only business I could see was the produce plant where I had worked for a day as a temporary laborer. I remembered it with disgust. The place was cold and drafty, the work hard and boring, and it had to be done standing up. The pay was minimum wage.

Thursday morning arrived, and I watched for her. It was cold again, and the wind made it worse. When I saw her turn the corner, the first thing I noticed was her smile.

It was back, and that made me feel good. The second thing I noticed was that she was wearing the gloves again.

"Good morning, Rose."

"Good morning, Pete." Her face changed, and the wrinkles got deeper. "I should apologize for yesterday. I do run on sometimes."

I tried to brush it off, not wanting her to dwell on her father's death. It was obviously a painful memory.

"I should never have told you that I don't eat peanut butter and jelly sandwiches."

I guess my face showed my surprise. "Excuse me?"

"I didn't stop to consider you might like them."

The answer didn't make any more sense than the apology. I found myself reverting to my earlier judgment—either she had Alzheimer's or she was crazy. I quietly acknowledged her apology, suddenly wondering about yesterday's tale. *Had that really happened, or was it something from an unstable mind?*

I noticed her reaching clumsily into her purse. What was she doing?

I had the answer almost immediately; she was holding her son's gloves. Rose carefully tucked them under one arm and reached back into her purse. This time, she clutched a man's leather wallet. She opened it, sadly smiled at what she saw, and then offered it to me to look. I couldn't refuse.

"That's my father on the left." I looked into the eyes of a large man with a big beer belly. Dwarfed in one huge arm was a little girl, her head against his, her arm trying to reach around his neck. Both were visibly laughing.

"And that's my son, Pete, on the right," she explained, her words directing my attention to the other picture. The man in the picture was terribly thin, his clothes hanging in limp folds. His scalp glistened from the flare of the flash. "Before he got cancer, he looked a lot like you. He died two weeks ago. It took a long time."

I glanced up from the picture, empty words of sympathy ready on my tongue. She rushed on before I could mouth them.

"Those pictures are all I have left of them. Those, and these gloves." They were back in her hand again, and she was holding them out to me. "Please, Pete, take them. I don't want to die with them. I want someone to live with them."

Humbled, I accepted them, just as the bus pulled up. It was early that day.

Rose didn't show up at the bus stop Friday morning.

I got my car back Saturday afternoon.

Monday morning, I drove by the bus stop. Rose wasn't there. She wasn't there Tuesday, either. She wasn't there the rest of the week.

I never saw her again.

Weeks later, when I finally told my mother about my experience, I found out that my father had a cousin he'd lost touch with. Her name was Rose. Her father's name was Pete, and so was her son's.

I still have the gloves. ❈

— PETE GRAFF

*I*n the Jewish tradition, marriages are big events. In fact, they are considered such major milestones that the celebrations don't stop with the matrimonial ceremony itself. During the week immediately following the wedding, special ritual feasts are held every night to extend the celebration. These seven nights are known as the *Sheva Brochos* (Seven Blessings), so called for the ritual benedictions that conclude the ceremony. Usually, these affairs are hosted by family members or close friends, who vie with one another for the honor of sponsoring the event. But what if the newly married couple comes from a small family, is new to the neighborhood, or doesn't know enough people to sponsor a week's worth of celebrations? Often, kindhearted strangers are asked to step in and take the place of the family members who aren't there.

Sarah Yeret Rosenblum was famous for her magnanimous spirit. So she took it in stride in June 1972 when she got a phone call asking her to "make *Sheva Brochos*" that night for two complete strangers. Today, she demurs about the physical and financial cost, modestly saying, "It wasn't any big deal, I wasn't being asked to give a million dollars away" — but any woman who has single-handedly hosted a dinner party for thirty strangers on sudden notice knows it's no easy feat.

Sarah Yeret immediately said yes, and for two good reasons: first, she was glad to do a *mitzvah* (a good deed); and second, the person who had asked her was someone she could never refuse. The call had come from Rabbi Shlomo Carlebach, the legendary "Singing Rabbi," known throughout the world for his emotional largesse as well as for his repertoire of thousands of popular Jewish melodies. It was typical of Shlomo to call someone at the last minute and ask him or her to under-take an act of kindness that others might well regard as burdensome. But he himself did it every minute of every single day of his life, so why shouldn't he expect others to sometimes do just a little bit of the same? Sarah looked up to Shlomo, admiring him immensely. She felt honored that he had asked *her* to be the host.

She got to work immediately, canvassing her Brooklyn neighborhood for extra chairs and tables. She rushed to local stores to buy food, paper goods, and a huge spotlight to illuminate the backyard where the party would be held. (Sarah herself was a relative new-lywed, and her apartment was too small to hold thirty people.) It took all day to prepare, but the *Sheva Brochos* was a huge success. There, Sarah met the newlyweds for the first time. Their names were Yehoshua and Emunah Witt, and they were very young and cute, stealing tender glances at one another throughout the evening. For years afterwards, Sarah vividly remembered the couple and the event. Everyone had had a wonderful time, and it had been a very proud moment for her. She had risen to a challenge, done something good, and helped launch a young couple's first week of marriage.

The next day, Yehoshua and Emunah left for Israel, and Sarah never saw them again. "I often wondered what had happened to them," she recalls, "but I myself moved out of town the following year and lost touch with Shlomo—our only link. On the rare occasions that I did speak with him, there was just too much catching up to do for me to remember to ask about the Witts. As far as I was concerned, they had disappeared off the face of this earth."

Fast forward twenty-five years. During this time Sarah had divorced, remarried, and was back in Brooklyn. Her eighteen-year-old daughter Avigayil was away in Israel for the year, studying at a women's Torah Institute in Sfat—the ancient Israeli city of mystics— located near the Galilee. Although Sarah worried about her daughter being so far from home, Avigayil reassured her that she was having a fabulous time. Her happiness was compounded by the fact that she had met a young woman named Sorala with whom she had developed an instant rapport and unusual camaraderie. "She's become my best friend," Avigayil told her mother over the phone, "and guess what? She's invited me to her home in Jerusalem for *Shabbat*. Sorala has a twin brother named Shmali, and she wants me to meet him. She's convinced that we're perfect for each other!"

There were lots of Sabbath guests at Sorala's home, and the family itself boasted fourteen children, which would have been enough to crowd any table—but that didn't hinder the patriarch of the family from engaging Avigayil in polite conversation and asking her about her life in America. Naturally, one of his first questions concerned her name, and he instantly began playing the six degrees of separation game—or, as it is more familiarly known in Israel, "Jewish geography."

"Yeret? Yeret?" he repeated, thoughtfully chewing on a piece of homemade *challah*. "Well, the only Yerets I ever met live in the States. Abraham and Sarah Yeret. You wouldn't be related to them by any chance, would you?"

"They're my parents!" Avigayil practically shrieked. "How do you know them?"

"They made our *Sheva Brochos*," Yehoshua Witt replied. "Twenty-five years ago . . ." And he began to reminisce about that fateful night when the Yerets' and the Witts' paths had crossed, and something stronger than destiny had been set into motion.

It seemed as if yet another wedding was soon in the offing. And this time it was the marriage of the Witts' son Shmali and the Yerets' daughter Avigayil that would be celebrated by the two families—and this time the two families would be present at *all* of the *Sheva Brochos* together, as their progeny were joined in holy matrimony.

"Little could I have imagined thirty years ago while setting the table for the Witts' *Sheva Brochos* that one day *their* offspring and mine would get married," Sarah says with a catch in her voice. "It almost seems as if Shmali and Avigayil's love was created before they were.

"I often wonder if Shlomo had any inkling about the forces he set into motion that night," Sarah ventures. "Sadly, he passed away in 1994, long before the kids' wedding in October 1997, but had he been alive I am sure he would have officiated.

"Actually, he *may* have had an intuition that Shmali and Avigayil's destinies were intertwined long before we did. When Shmali and Avigayil began trading stories and sharing pieces of their past together as young couples always do, they discovered that their paths had crossed once before.

"In the summer of 1988, Shlomo Carlebach performed at a huge *Klezmer* concert in Sfat, and Shmali was up on stage with him, singing backup. Suddenly, Shlomo looked into the crowd and his eyes lit on an excited little girl standing nearby. He pulled her up onto the stage and placed her next to Shmali. And do you know who that young girl was standing next to Shmali on Shlomo's stage in 1988?

"That girl was Avigayil."

—SARAH ROSENBLUM

When I told my husband Dave that I was pregnant, I expected a surprised but happy reaction. I was sadly mistaken.

The news hit him like a wrecking ball, and his words swung back at me just as hard: "Oh, that's just *@%# great."

I was crushed. I was expecting something more along the lines of: "Oh babe, that's awesome!" or even a dumbfounded "How . . . ?"

Yet his words were full of anger and contempt. I kept my cool that night, deciding that he had been caught off guard. I felt sure that his nasty response would soon give way to excitement and anticipation. However, the weeks went by and he still wasn't coming around. Family and close friends told me he was just afraid of this new responsibility, and probably didn't feel he was "ready" to become a dad.

Well, too bad, I thought. We were "ready."

A great deal of Dave's bitterness stemmed from the fact that we had planned on waiting one more year before starting our family. Things accidentally got "bumped ahead" of schedule, I told him.

Aside from Dave, I was enjoying every moment of my pregnancy. Not a touch of morning sickness or problems of any sort. I could've done cartwheels for the whole nine months! I read every book I could get my hands on and watched every episode of *Baby Story* on the Learning Channel. I was completely absorbed in the miracle of life going on inside me. What a gift! I wished Dave would share the joy with me.

I came up with an idea I thought might work: a childbirth education course. If he saw other couples in the same boat, he might get into it, right? He came with me to the first class, and to my delight, he participated in the discussions and didn't act as if I had dragged him there. Well, that was a one-shot deal.

The following week he came home late and said he couldn't be ready to go to the class in time. I totally lost it. After screaming and yelling at him for being such a you-know-what, I decided I would stay home and make his life miserable. I wasn't about to show up alone!

Then I completely changed my mind. With class set to start in less than five minutes, I flew out of the house by myself and drove like crazy to the class.

Mercifully, it wasn't a class where you practice labor positions with your spouse. It was all about budgeting and preparing financially for your baby. To me, the woman lecturing sounded like Charlie Brown's teacher.

I tuned out and spent the hour looking around the room at the other parents-to-be, wondering in frustration what had caused my husband to turn into such a jerk.

Then I snapped out of my reverie and heard the teacher say that it is an excellent idea to get life insurance when you start a family. *Hey, that's probably a good point,* I thought. And then, zap, I went back to my bitter thoughts.

By the time I got home, I realized that despite all the information relayed during the class, the only thing I had taken away was the fact that maybe we should look at life insurance. Of course, I didn't say anything to Dave that night, as I was giving him the silent treatment.

Once we were back on speaking terms, we agreed that life insurance was a good idea. A medical representative from the insurance company came to our house, questioned us, weighed us, and took samples of our blood and urine. We signed some papers, figured it was just a matter of waiting for the monthly premiums to start coming out of our bank account, and thought nothing more of it.

Then Anna was born. We had no idea what a beautiful transformation our lives would undergo as a result of her birth. She came at the end of June and she completely took over our hearts. Both of us were consumed with love as soon as we saw her chubby pink body. Dave completely metamorphosed. After nine months of uncertainty, I saw him embrace fatherhood and I knew that everything was going to be all right.

And then it happened. Less than a week after Anna was born we received a rejection letter from the insurance company. Dave had failed the medical exam. At the bottom in bold letters was a note explaining that protein had been detected in his urine, and that he should get to a doctor immediately.

Baffled, he went to a walk-in clinic that day. They took his blood pressure—which was sky high—followed by myriad blood and urine tests. The doctor told my husband straight out that he suspected it was kidney failure. Following an ultrasound test and a kidney biopsy, it was confirmed that Dave had less than 15 percent kidney function in both of his kidneys.

We quickly learned more than we ever wanted to know about kidneys and kidney disease. Dave's particular kidney disease was called IGA-nephropathy. Put simply, the filters in his kidneys were semi-plugged and couldn't keep up with their job of filtering the toxins out of his body. I visualized a backed-up sink that wouldn't let the dirty water down.

The doctors speculated that Dave had acquired the condition because he was born prematurely. His kidneys were not yet developed but were forced to start working anyway. Their degeneration had probably been happening for many years, and they were finally starting to show the strain. In fact, they were barely slugging along.

Dave had not known that anything was the matter because his body didn't know anything different. He had never known what it felt like to have 100 percent kidney function. He had no clue that he was ill.

I watched my husband and his parents cry as the nurse explained dialysis; the medications that would be prescribed for him; the diet he had to follow; and the kidney transplant that would be imminent.

Dave's father was a perfect match and he generously donated one of his kidneys. He gave his son life once, and had now given it to him again. The transplant surgery took place on September 11, 2002, of all days. September 11 is a day of great sorrow for many, but for us it is also a day of great hope.

I can't forget to mention Anna. Our little sunshine. She saved her daddy. It is quite possible that Dave could have continued on unaware of his condition and could eventually have collapsed and died of kidney failure. I'm sure glad that God didn't wait for Dave to be "ready" to be a dad! ❦

— LEANNE WILKINSON

oday, there are a growing number of Orthodox Jews in the Israeli army, but decades ago their presence was rare. Devoted to rabbinical studies day and night, many acquired exemptions from the government that released them from the country's legal requirement to serve for three years. Consequently, in the past, almost all Israeli soldiers were bareheaded and nonobservant Jews, devout in their dedication to their people but less stringent in their adherence to Jewish law.

Ari Ben-David*, twenty-two years old, was a typical Israeli solder in that he was nonobservant like most of his comrades. He was *atypical*, however, by virtue of the fact that he was Canadian-born and had recently emigrated to the Jewish state. He was full of Zionistic fire and fervently wanted to serve his newly adopted country. So he joined the army in 1981 and was assigned to "*Handasa Kaarvit*," the "Combat Engineer" unit, otherwise known as the "zappers." This was the tank division that moved forward in advance of the rest of the troops, rooting out land mines and booby traps, defusing explosives, and in general preparing fresh areas for the incursions of Israeli troops. In 1982, Ari Ben-David's unit was sent to the Shuf Mountains in Lebanon, where it ran smack into an armored forces unit of the Syrian army. Thus, the longest and most intense battle in the Lebanon war—"*Ain Zachleta*"—was launched, and Ari Ben-David, a young, idealistic, fresh-faced kid from Canada, was caught in the thick of it.

"Really fierce fighting ensued," he remembers. "Many of the skirmishes turned out to be life-or-death propositions. Sometimes we hung on by the skin of our teeth. But it was never each man for himself. Throughout the entire conflict, we all looked out for one another, and took risks to save each other's lives. We were all in this together."

Barricaded inside their tanks, the young soldiers were isolated from one another. "I had no idea who my other comrades were," Ari says. "But ultimately it didn't matter. We were fighting for our country, each other, and our very own lives."

As the battle heated up, Ari couldn't help but notice that one particular tank seemed to always be at *his* tank's side.

"This tank was always parallel to ours. Somehow, as we advanced, this one tank advanced in tandem with us. During skirmishes tanks tend to get detached from one another and don't necessarily fight side-by-side. We were *not* assigned to be near one another. But as the days unfolded, this particular tank just constantly seemed to be right next to ours. And as it turned out, we worked well with each other. There were times when that tank covered for us, shielded us, warded off the snipers shooting at us from the trees, was outright responsible for saving our lives. And there were times when we returned the favor. Somehow our two tanks had fallen into an informal 'buddy' system, although not a word ever passed between our men and theirs. It just happened."

Ari saw the tank next to him so many times throughout the five-day ordeal at *Ain Zachleta* that he memorized the unit number marked onto its surface: *"Aleph Two."* And, even though he couldn't see the other two soldiers inside the tank, he did often glimpse the young tank comander's head bobbing up on top. During quiet interludes, he would wave "hello" or "thanks" to the commander. He had never met him before and had no clue as to his name. But his face would forever be engraved on his memory. The commander was responsible for saving his life on more than one occasion, and he, in turn, had saved his.

Five days later, the battle of *Ain Zachleta* was over and Ari was sent elsewhere. He never had a chance to personally meet the other tank commander nor to thank him for saving his life. During the entire time, they had not exchanged a single word.

In 1983, Ari's three years of service with the army came to an end. And then a period of intense searching for meaning and inner peace began. Ari was launched on his own personal voyage of discovery. He left Israel, traveled around, got married, got divorced, moved to various states in America, tried out different jobs and identities, and finally realized that what he wanted out of life was a more intense brand of Judaism than he had previously embraced. Ari started studying Judaism in a serious way and became a returnee (*"baal teshuva"*). In 2001, Ari moved to Brooklyn and married again, this time to an Orthodox Jewish woman with whom he could live an observant life. He was introduced to her extended family, who were religious Jews.

Ten months after they were married, Ari and his wife traveled to Queens, New York, to visit his wife's sister and brother-in-law. As they conversed pleasantly in the living room, Ari's eyes started roving around the room, and he caught sight of a photograph that he had not noticed in his previous visits to his new in-laws.

"Who's this?" he asked casually, pointing to a young, bareheaded Israeli soldier in uniform.

"Oh, that's Uri," his wife's sister told him lightly. "My dear husband, your beloved brother-in-law."

"You're kidding!" Ari shook his head in disbelief as his eyes strayed to Uri Kahan, his now-observant brother-in-law, in full Orthodox Jewish regalia (yarmulke, beard, and conservative garb).

"Uri, I didn't know you were in the Israeli army!"

"Hey," Uri shrugged dismissively, "it's no big deal. All native-born Israelis are required to serve. You know

I'm a *Sabra* (native-born Israeli), right? Anyway, it was a lifetime ago. Almost twenty years ago, in fact, long before I became an observant Jew and emigrated to New York."

"Well, we have something in common then, besides our wives," Ari said lightly. "Did I ever tell you that I *also* served in the Israeli army?"

"You're *Canadian.* What were you doing in the army? No, you never mentioned it before."

"You know," Ari stared harder at the photograph, "there's something about this photograph that's familiar. "*When* were you in the army?"

"1981 to '83."

"What a coincidence! So was I! What unit were you in?"

"The *Handasa Kaarvit.*"

"Me, too!"

The two men looked at each other in growing excitement.

"Wait a second!" Ari exclaimed as a memory stirred his mind. "Were you ever in the famous battle of *Ain Zachleta* in the Shuf Mountains?"

"Whew! I sure was! That was the most intense five-day period in my service. It was touch and go. We were in tremendous peril throughout."

"You don't by any chance remember your tank number, do you?" Ari pressed.

"Sure I do," Uri replied. *"Aleph Two."*

"And you were the commander, right?" Ari said.

"Now, how would you know that?" Uri stared at Ari in shock.

"Because I used to wave at you throughout the day. And we saved each other's lives several times over the course of that one long battle . . . Uri, allow me to reintroduce myself to you, not as your brother-in-law but as your comrade in arms. Hello, Uri, I'm Assistant Commander Ari Ben-David, tank number *Beit Three*. The tank that seemed almost cojoined to *yours* through that famous battle.

"I've always wanted to meet the man who saved my life so many times. But I never dreamed that if I ever found him, he would turn out to be my brother-in-law!" ✾

—ARI BEN-DAVID

*F*or most parents with young children, the month of October is spent obsessing about the perfect Halloween costume and paying way too much for a pumpkin. It's about trick-or-treat parties, nonpermanent makeup, and gooey, gruesome props. In other words, it's the kind of holiday most parents look forward to, and by the look of some costumes, live for. It's one of those Kodak moments for parents. I'd be one of those parents myself if it weren't for one snag—my son Alex is autistic and he hasn't a clue as to what Halloween is all about. Taking Alex to a pumpkin patch is like giving him a giant maze to run through—only he doesn't watch where he is going, so he ends up falling over and crashing into pumpkins, mutant giant squash, and just about anything else in the field. Alex is also allergic to hay and straw, so it takes only about ten minutes for his eyes to bulge out, followed by intense itching, wheezing, and a quick trip back home.

Every year I'd begin the month of October by saying to Alex, "Let's read a Halloween story." I had books depicting all of his favorite characters: Barney, Winnie the Pooh, Elmo, etc., in various stages of trick-or-treat bliss. I showed him pictures of pumpkins, witches, ghosts, black cats, and anything else I could find to get him interested in the holiday. Alex memorized the pictures and pointed to them on command. We listened to Halloween music, watched videos, and went to costume stores. I'd ask him, "What costume do you want? What do you want to be for Halloween?"

No response. Alex is nine years old. He has a vocabulary of fewer than fifty words, most of them one-syllable, and he rarely makes eye contact.

When Alex was one, we started out with a big pumpkin, but as the years passed, the pumpkins got smaller. I knew that if Alex didn't show an interest soon, the shrinking pumpkin would turn into no pumpkin. I had the choice of not celebrating this holiday, but I did it anyhow. When Alex was five, I put a fireman's hat and coat on him, stuck a plastic pumpkin in his hand, and dragged him up and down the block. I did this because Alex lacked social skills. I wanted to provide him with what the neighborhood kids had—a shot at some candy and a good time. Perhaps I wanted for me what the other neighborhood moms had—a shot at something normal. I knew that it would not work out that way. I was using Halloween as a chance to teach social skills and I hated doing it, but I had no choice because I didn't want Alex to remain trapped inside himself.

As we came to each house I said, "Alex, time to ring the bell."

Then the battle began.

He screamed, "Noooooo!"

I held him by the hand and walked him up the stairs to the *front* door of each home and said firmly, "OK, we'll ring the bell together."

I took his finger in my hand and placed it on the bell. The sound of the bells seemed to quiet Alex, as if he knew something was going to happen. The door would open and out would pop a cheerful neighbor, who was usually full of questions: "Where did you get your costume? What kind of candy do you want?" I'd reply for Alex, and add, "He has trouble speaking." I knew all the questions, yet each time, I felt unprepared to answer.

Alex had a little picture symbol that had "trick or treat" on one side and "thank you" on the other. I pinned it to the lapel of his fireman's costume and directed him to point to one side, and then turn the picture over to the other side in response to the questions. This was supposed to be a stab at independent communication, but it was turning out to be more like a lesson in futility. Alex would either push the candy bowl away, or pick up a piece of candy and stare intensely at it while turning it between his thumb and forefinger, and then put it back in approximately the same place. Sometimes, he would hand the candy back. I'd say, "He's not much of a candy eater, but thank you anyway," and off we'd go. I was particularly disappointed when he gave back the chocolate.

Our next-door neighbor, Eva, had arranged a beautiful candy platter with a miniature pumpkin in the middle. Alex grabbed the pumpkin and tossed it in his plastic container. When I tried to get it out, Eva said, "He can have it." Tired and cold, I thanked her and dragged Alex down the steps and to the corner. "One more block . . . just one more block," I said to him, but I was really just saying it to the moon.

By the fifth house, Alex stopped protesting. I don't know why. Alex and I, desperately in need of a flashlight and a tissue for our runny noses, met up with a mom and her daughter who obliged us with both. "What a pretty princess," I said to the little girl. She looked about five and had long blond hair that was pushed back into an upright ponytail, held in place with what looked like three or four pink ribbons, the ends of which cascaded to her shoulders. Of course, there was a sequined crown, a magic wand, and a long, silky pink dress that reached to her sneakers. She had on "little-girl lipstick," the color of pink cotton candy, and her cheeks were rosy, probably more from the cold than from the makeup. "Say thank you," said her mother, and the little girl replied, "Thank you," and made her way to the next house.

Her mother watched from the sidewalk as we all went to each house. I let the little princess ring the bells and say the line. This made it easier for me, and for Alex, who was now enjoying the clonking sound the candy made as it hit the bottom of his pumpkin. It was close to eight o'clock, and some of the neighbors were starting to give only one piece of candy to the children because they didn't want to run out. Alex followed the little princess, and I followed behind him in a straight line with her mother at my side.

I watched from the sidewalk while the princess and Alex walked up the steps to a house that looked mostly dark, with just an inch of light peering out from under the kitchen curtains. The princess rang once, twice, then three times, but nobody answered. As she turned to walk away, she let out an exhausted cry, and looked down at her bag that was only half filled.

At that moment—which took no more than a second—Alex reached into his plastic pumpkin, took out a candy, and tossed it in her bag.

The little girl watched the candy fall into place with the others, glanced up at Alex in a confused sort of way, and walked down the steps to her mother. It was dark, so I don't even think the mother saw the incident. Alex followed suit, and when he came to me, I didn't say a word. I just wrapped my arms around him. I knew it was time to head home—and Alex was more than ready. As we walked back to the house in silence, I thought about what I had just witnessed.

That moment is etched in my mind. I am grateful that there was no photograph, no video, no instant replay that might prove me wrong. Autism is a neurological disorder of the brain that remains a mystery. That mystery is my son Alex. He taught me to never blink twice. ❀

—DIANA M. MARTIN

A few years ago, my wife and I were persuaded by friends to help an organization providing meals for pensioners who were housebound and without families to celebrate Christmas Day. We were glad to do so, although, in truth, I found the whole thing a bit of a disappointment. Secretly, I suppose, I expected them to be jolly, chuckling gray-haired grannies and grandpas, blinking away tears of gratitude as we played out our fantasy of Lord and Lady Bountiful.

Forget it! These people were made of sterner stuff. "You're late!" was the first greeting I received.

"You call this Christmas pudding?" or "this gravy is cold" or "last year we had three of these!" From apartment to apartment they were, to borrow loosely from P. G. Wodehouse, if not actually disgruntled, far from being actively gruntled!

As always, Inka, my wife, got it right when I grumbled that they could at least be more grateful. "What are you talking about?" she said.

"We're doing this to make *them* feel a little better, not *you*. Most have been abandoned by their families at a time when they really need them. After a lifetime of work, they are left with little money and precious few comforts. We turn up on Christmas Day with a meal and a can of Guinness, and you want them to be grateful?" Still, nothing prepared even *her* for our encounter with Kathleen and her sister Hilly.

In their early seventies, they had shared the same poky little apartment for forty years, the last thirty of which were notable for the fact that neither had exchanged a single word with the other. They moved around the same small space they jointly occupied as if the other simply didn't exist. It was, to put it mildly, weird and ineffably sad.

Never a "good morning" or a "hello" or a "please pass the salt." They spoke to everyone else but not to each other, not once, and, as far as they were concerned, not ever again.

I once asked Kathleen what it was that had come between them. She told me a long story involving their mother and a brooch. I then asked Hilly. The brooch was also mentioned but so was a trip to Westcliff-on-Sea. I couldn't make it out at all and wondered whether *they* did any more. So why didn't they live apart? That was also part of the standoff. Both were damned if they were the one who ought to move, so for thirty years they had lived in this state of distressing enmity. Much against my advice, Inka decided to "adopt" them.

That involved going to see them once a month and taking them out two or three times a year, on holidays, including, of course, Christmas.

Candidly, these were not occasions to which I looked forward. Hilly was all right, though getting her out of the apartment was invariably a nightmare as she debated, seemingly for hours, whether to wear her white jumper or her blue. We once, unthinkingly, made the mistake of buying her a pink one, thus compounding the problem.

Kathleen was another matter.

Whenever I see the word "cantankerous" I think of her. No one I have ever met can wind me up so effortlessly.

We took them to see *Cats*. At supper afterwards, Kathleen hissed, "I suppose you know that friend of yours, Andrew Lloyd Webber (I'd made the mistake of saying I knew him) stole that song, 'Memory'?"

"I don't think he did, Kathleen," I said, trying hard to conceal my irritation.

"Oh, yes, I've heard it many times. Your friend just picked it up and plunked it in his show."

"No," I said. "You heard it before because the show has been running for many years. No one says that tonight is the first time it has ever been sung. Lots of singers have sung it."

"Well, there you are," she said with a note of triumph. "You must admit it then. He stole it."

Inka gave me a "just let it drop" look but I bickered on just as I did a few months later when we took them out to a meal and to my intense surprise Kathleen chose spaghetti as a starter.

"This is not spaghetti," she announced to the entire restaurant when a plate of what couldn't be anything other than spaghetti arrived.

"What is it then?" I asked with some asperity.

"This is pasta," she said. "What I want is spaghetti. Spaghetti comes in hoops, something which I'd have thought even *you* would know. This is pasta and I don't eat pasta."

But for all Kathleen's obduracy and Hilly's jumper problems, there was something special about them both. Though I found it all too easy to be irritated by them, I couldn't remain cross for long.

In any case, the balance of power suddenly and subtly shifted. Inka became very ill and the sisters, quite separately and sweetly, decided that now we needed *their* help. This change of circumstances suited them perfectly. Over the years they had been ground down by poverty and misfortune and had become the "clients" of our British Social Security system.

It didn't suit them. Now, suddenly, they had the opportunity to give rather than to receive and, within the limitations of their own ill health, both did wonderfully well. One day, Hilly said she thought she might have the solution to Inka's problem. Never underestimate, she told us, the power of prayer.

She announced that she'd be taking Inka to Midnight

Mass at Westminster Cathedral that Christmas. When I told Kathleen about these plans she snorted.

"That's not for me," she said. "You come around and I'll make you your favorite meal."

"What's my favorite meal?" I asked, fearing the worst.

"Spaghetti," she said. "The real stuff in the tins."

So off to the cathedral they went—Hilly and Inka—Hilly taking less time than normal to choose her jumper, almost unnaturally excited. Cardinal Basil Hume, alas no longer with us, presided.

"He gave me a good look," Hilly whispered to Inka in the church. "He was very nice."

"I told you pink suited you," Inka replied.

They came back to the apartment, where Kathleen and I were engaged in a bad-tempered game of gin rummy. Hilly took off her coat, put down her handbag, and walked over to Kathleen. "You should have come with us, dear, it was lovely. Anyway, Happy Christmas, dear." And she smiled, a beatific smile.

Nobody moved. It was like one of those film freeze-frames. I sat with my cards in my hand. Inka leaned against the door, her mouth open.

Hilly just stood there with that smile.

And Kathleen, ah, Kathleen: One sensed she had trouble breathing.

Then she turned her head away and I'm willing to swear, though she would forever deny it, that I saw a single tear glistening in her eye.

Then, breaking the spell, she stood up as if nothing had happened; as if this was not the most momentous day for both of them in thirty years; as if talking was always for them the most natural thing in the world; and she said: "Oh come on, Hilly, you daft old thing, you know I don't go in for all that nonsense. Now come with me, we've got the washing up to do."

And they haven't stopped talking since.

Now don't get me wrong. I don't believe in miracles, especially not Christmas miracles. All I'm saying is that something very peculiar and very wonderful happened on that Christmas night. Inka says that in the very act of seeking help for someone else's problems, Hilly discovered the solution to her own. Prayer has that power, she says.

I don't seek explanations. It happened, that's all. On that Christmas Day, Kathleen and Hilly, who were lost, found each other again. ✤

Reprinted with permission from the *London Daily Mail*, Sunday, December 23, 2001, by Steven Steward, "If this wasn't a miracle, what was it?"

*T*wo strangers sat side by side on a British Airways flight to New York, barely speaking. Around them the cacophony that usually explodes on international flights filled the air: wails of children, rounds of laughter, excited chatter. There is something about a long flight that inspires camaraderie. But the men sitting in seats 12A and 12B were stonily silent, in contrast to everyone else around them.

No one would have given a single thought to the possibility that anything out of the ordinary was about to occur between these two men as they first settled into their seats. Joshua Stein,* a yarmulke-wearing Orthodox Jew from London, warmly extended his hand in amiable greeting to his seatmate, a nonobservant American Jew. The American grumpily took his hand, shook it limply and without enthusiasm, nodded perfunctorily, and barked out his name: Marc Kimpfheimer.* Joshua tried valiantly to engage the other man in pleasant conversation, but the man was unreceptive. He seemed to have an "attitude." Joshua shrugged his shoulders and pulled out a Bible to study. Around him the aisles were buzzing with heated political debates, topical gossip, and idle conversation. It would be a lonely six-hour flight.

Joshua was a perceptive person and a sensitive man, to boot. He had never met Marc before and wondered why he was so curt. It troubled him that, at such a precarious time in contemporary history, human beings should be unfriendly to one another. Finally, he couldn't take it anymore. He turned to Marc and asked abruptly, "Tell me, why are you so hostile to me? Have we ever met before?"

Marc dropped his semi-polite facade and became outright surly. "Sorry," he said, "but I just can't stand religion and religious Jews. Just leave me alone, OK?"

Joshua Stein was taken aback by Marc Kimpfheimer's rude remark, but tried to transcend it. He realized that something must have deeply hurt this man and that there was a deep underlying reason for his rage. So, instead of withdrawing from the man as others in his situation would have done, Joshua put his hand gently on Marc's shoulder and said, "Please tell me what happened."

Startled by Joshua's unexpected reaction and compassionate manner, Marc began unburdening himself. He had been a young married man in Europe right before the outbreak of World War II. He had loved his wife Babshi* dearly, and they had a child named Itsikl.* Marc was deeply devoted to his family and they were his world.

When the Nazis overran his small town in Poland, all

the Jews were rounded up and marched to the outskirts of town. The men were separated from their wives and children and forced to dig enormous pits all day long. When they finished their work, the Nazis assembled the women and children near the pit and started shooting. Marc watched in horror as the shots rang out, felling his wife and Itsikl. He watched them topple into the pit.

"This is how God pays back religious Jews?" he shouted at Joshua. "This is a good God, a benevolent God, a God who loves His people? Bah! There is no God! If my wife and son, the purest souls on this earth, could die like that, I don't want to know such a God!"

Marc had never remarried or built another family. It was more than forty years later, but in his mind he had never left the Holocaust. He was, instead, frozen in time.

Joshua was deeply moved by Marc's story. He tried to reach out to him by alternately comforting him and explaining why God was not dead and how to understand the Holocaust from a religious perspective. While Marc was more courteous to Joshua for the rest of the trip, he was hostile to all talk of religious philosophy and viewpoint. For the rest of the flight, Joshua talked to him of minor things that would not provoke his anger or exacerbate his pain. When they reached their destination—JFK Airport in New York—Joshua bid Marc farewell, certain he would never see him again.

Seven months later, Joshua Stein was in Israel to mark the High Holidays. Every year he traveled from his home in London to Jerusalem to observe Rosh Hashanah and Yom Kippur. He felt his religious experience would be more intense if he spent it in the sacred city drenched in holiness.

On Yom Kippur—the holiest day in the Jewish calendar—Joshua's synagogue in the Katamon section of Jerusalem had just given congregants a traditional break in between services. While some worshipers rushed home to catch a brief nap that might offer them respite from their fasting headaches, Joshua Stein decided to get a breath of fresh air instead. He was taking a brief walk near the synagogue when he noticed a bareheaded man, dressed in casual wear, sitting on a park bench, smoking a cigarette—which flouted the laws of Yom Kippur. As Joshua approached, the man brazenly raised his cigarette higher in the air, taunting him with his clear defiance of Jewish law. Obviously, this man had not been inside a synagogue that day.

Joshua was troubled by the man's lack of reverence and respect, and impulsively decided it was incumbent upon him to give him a little *musar* (lecture). As he reached the park bench, however, he was startled to realize that the man was none other than Marc—his seatmate from the British Airways flight.

After they exchanged startled greetings, Joshua tried to coax Marc into joining him at his synagogue.

"Do you lack a brain?" the cantankerous old man shouted. "I told you on the plane how I feel about God!"

But Joshua was inspired. "Well, OK, yes, don't come for God. But do you know that we're having a break right now, and right after the break, the congregation will be saying the *Yizkor*—the memorial service for the dead? Have you ever honored your beloved wife and son by chanting those prayers in their memory? You don't have to stay for the rest of the services. But shouldn't you at least say a prayer for them?"

Marc displayed a twinge of guilt. He had not considered that he might be dishonoring his wife's and child's memory by not intoning the memorial prayers.

"I'll come in just for the memorial prayers," he told Joshua, "but just that. The minute the *Yizkor* is over, I'm outta there!"

"Fine. Just come with me now."

Joshua was jubilant that Marc was accompanying him to the synagogue. By his own admission, Marc had not been inside a synagogue for over forty years.

As he escorted Marc inside the synagogue, Joshua felt overcome by what had occurred and by his own personal sense of responsibility. He wanted this synagogue experience to be a positive one for his new acquaintance, and, despite his protestations, the beginning—*not* the end—of a reconnection with his Jewish roots. He was determined to make the experience a meaningful and memorable one for Marc.

First, he took Marc around to many of the congregants and introduced him. They all welcomed him

warmly into their fold. Then, Joshua approached the
Baal Tefillah, the man who was leading the prayer services that day, and asked him if he would make an
announcement in the shul, welcoming Marc. He quickly
explained the situation and stressed how much he
wanted Marc to feel comfortable. Then Joshua made an
unusual request of the prayer leader. He asked him to
publicly intone a special *Kel Rachaman* (one of the
prayers of the *Yizkor* service) for Marc's lost family. The
prayer leader agreed, and the *Yizkor* was commenced.

When the prayer leader reached the special *Kel
Rachaman* memorial prayer, he realized he did not know
the names of Marc's family members (which must be
inserted into the prayer). He tiptoed over to Marc and
asked for the names he needed to recite. When Marc
answered that his son's name was Itsikl ben (the son of)
Babshi, and his wife's was Babshi bas (the daughter of)
Fruma Sorah, the prayer leader blanched momentarily.
Then he strode to the pulpit and intoned the prayer.

Despite his best attempts to maintain a cool,
detached distance, the tears fell copiously from Marc's
eyes as he chanted the memorial prayers. All the grief,
misery, mourning, and loss that had been bottled up
inside him spilled onto the pages of the worn prayerbook
he held in his hand. His shoulders heaved in wrenching
sobs as he vocalized the names of his wife Babshi and his
son Itsikl. How he had loved them! How he missed
them! The pain—almost forty years later—was still too

much to bear. His anger at God began to bubble up to the surface once again. When the *Yizkor* service was over, he tried to slip unobtrusively out the door.

But the *Baal Tefillah* stopped Marc as he was about to leave.

"I need to ask you something," he said. "Mr. Stein told me your first name, and during *Yizkor* you told me your wife's and child's first names, too. But nobody told me your last name. Can you tell me please, what it is?"

"My last name?" Marc rolled his eyes, wondering why the man was asking with such urgency. "Kimpfheimer," he answered shortly. "*Chag Sameach* (Happy Holiday)."

Although Marc wanted to leave, he couldn't—the prayer leader had just turned a terrifying chalk-white and fainted on the floor.

"What's the matter with him?" Marc asked the men who rushed to help him. "Is he a bad faster?"

But when the prayer leader returned to consciousness, it was his turn to give Marc the shock of his life.

"Allow me to introduce myself," he whispered softly. "I am Itsikl ben Babshi. Your son."

"No, it's not true! You're lying! You're playing a terrible prank on me!" Marc screamed. "How could you do this to me—an old man, barely alive?"

"I know what a shock this must be for you, as it is for me," Itsikl said compassionately to Marc, placing a gentle hand on this shoulder. "All these years, I thought you were dead. . . ."

"B-but," Marc stammered, suddenly noticing how much this man, also no longer young, resembled his wife. "I saw . . . with my own two eyes . . . you and your mother fall into the pit after the bullets rang out. I saw you both crumple . . . dead."

"That is true," said the prayer leader gently. "We both fell into the pit. But my mother fell on top of me and shielded me from the bullet. She died. I lived." ❀

*S*everal weeks after our beloved father died in 1984, my sister Miriam came to stay at my house, which was vacant for the weekend. (My husband, my son, and I had gone upstate.) She shared an apartment with a roommate, and immediately after our father's death she needed a little more space and quiet to grieve in. Our departure that weekend was fortuitous for her, and she gratefully seized my offer to stay in our home while we were absent.

We had been shattered by our father's sudden death, and my sister was devastated. She needed some respite, and, hopefully, the healing that solitude might provide. She opened the door to my home with the key I had given her, and she dropped her bags on the living room floor. Then she was drawn into the kitchen to gaze fondly at the photograph of our father that was displayed on a ledge over the kitchen sink. It stood on one of those old-fashioned shelves or mantels that most women adorn with knickknacks and figurines. Inside the small space I had wedged a plaque bearing my father's photograph and a poignant poem he had once written, and it had remained securely moored there since his death.

From afar, my sister looked at the photograph tenderly, felt the inevitable tears well up in her eyes, and hurriedly left the kitchen to gather up her bags. But as soon as she entered the living room, she heard a loud thud coming from the kitchen. She returned to the kitchen, wondering what had caused the noise, and stared in astonishment at the plaque. It was no longer standing firmly embedded inside the snug, enclosed ledge. Instead, it was now—inexplicably—lying on the kitchen floor.

Miriam couldn't understand what had suddenly made the plaque plummet to the floor. It had been virtually pinned inside the deep and small space; it was not as if it had been precariously perched on the edge of the shelf. She wondered what had made it fall. No heavy trucks rumbled outside, nor were there any men with machinery working nearby. The sun shone brightly, and there was no hint of an approaching storm. As part of an attached house, our kitchen had no apertures in it, so the happening couldn't possibly have been caused by a sudden gust of wind rattling the windows. Neither could it have resulted from a tiny earthquake, because everything else in the room was in order. No sounds were being emitted from my neighbors' apartments; I had, in fact, warned Miriam that both my upstairs and downstairs tenants were away for the summer and that she would be completely alone in the building. There was simply no way to account for the plaque on the floor.

My sister picked up the plaque, returned it to its place on the shelf, and made sure that, once again, it was deeply embedded inside. Then she returned to the living room to gather up her bags once more. No sooner had she stepped out of the kitchen than the plaque fell to the floor a second time.

Miriam's eyes grew large in shock as she examined my father's photograph—on the floor, again. She was a big-time skeptic, but she was beginning to get spooked. "OK, Dad, are you trying to tell me something?" she addressed the photograph in mock consternation as she retrieved it a second time. She was punctilious in ascertaining that the plaque was tightly secured in its space before she returned to her bags in the living room.

But seconds later, the plaque inexplicably plunged to the floor a third time, and my terrified sister picked up her pocketbook and fled. She was too shaken to return that weekend.

The plaque has remained in my home for nineteen years, and it has never fallen once in all this time—neither before the incident with my sister, nor after. My sister was the "baby" of the family upon whom my father doted, and she suffered tremendously after his death. To this day, we are all convinced that my father was trying to communicate with her—but since she retreated too quickly, the message remains unclear. ❀

—YITTA HALBERSTAM

I have always believed in the power of dreams. God spoke to many people in the Bible through dreams, and there is no reason why he should stop now!

In 1998, my grandfather died unexpectedly. He was seventy-nine, and I should have been psychologically able to let him go, but I shuddered to think of a world without him. You see, he wasn't an ordinary Gramps.

I came from a small town in Missouri and was raised by my mother and half-sister. There was no man in our house. We were very close emotionally and physically to my maternal grandparents, who lived next door. Gramps was always there. He and I had our own special outing together every Saturday morning. He would teach me about the beauty of nature—pointing out birds' nests, trees, and clouds. He taught me how to play golf, go camping, and drive a car. We did the father-daughter campouts and dances. He walked me down the aisle. Life without Gramps was unthinkable. But, being a nurse, I found it impossible not to notice that his health was declining. He had already been through a quintuple heart bypass eleven years before. I sort of felt that those eleven years were a gift, allowing Gramps to see my two sons born and watch them grow. They got closer to Gramps. Although we lived two hours away, we visited each other often.

On the day of his final heart attack, he had played eighteen holes of golf, mown the front and back lawns, and done some woodworking on a special picture frame in the swelteringly hot workroom. Gramps didn't know he was having another heart attack. He thought he was getting bronchitis. He treated himself for two days before letting us know he was ill.

Things moved quickly after that. Since he was too sick to be transferred to a larger, better equipped hospital, he got the best care the small-town hospital could offer. After two days of watching his condition worsen, I insisted that he be transferred—even though I knew it wouldn't help. Still, I had to try. Gramps died shortly after arriving at the second hospital, in the midst of all the best that medical technology had to offer. It just was his time.

Gramps's death devastated me. For a couple of weeks, I felt like I would never be normal again. There would always be a big hole in my heart. Gramps loved me because I was me. Nobody will ever love me like that again. That is not to say I'm not loved by others, but Gramps was special. His death also affected my children deeply. Three weeks before Gramps died, my husband's mother — Nana — succumbed after a long bout with cancer.

Losing both Nana and Gramps in the same month created a tremendous burden of grief for my seven- and nine-year-old boys. My younger son, Josh, seemed to be particularly in touch with my feelings. When my husband told the children that Gramps had died, Josh came directly to my bedside, put his arm around me, and said, "I'm *sooo* sorry." His eyes met mine and he said, "But he's in heaven now," and then he went on his little seven-year-old way. I thought how much he didn't understand my grief and how much more complicated things were when you were grown-up. At the funeral, Josh took a little angel lapel pin — one that I had given him at Nana's funeral — and pinned it on Gramps's lapel. He said he wanted Gramps to have it. I was beginning to think that Josh understood more than I had given him credit for. Then the miracle happened.

In a fitful night of sleep, about two weeks later, I dreamed I was crying. I was screaming in an open field — much like the ones Gramps and I had walked through many times. In the distance were a few trees, but they looked scrawny, as it was fall and high winds had already whipped many leaves off their branches. I cried out: "Gramps, I need to see you!" I lay down in the field, weeping uncontrollably. Suddenly, a single red leaf blew over to me — just a solitary one. I picked it up, and I knew that Gramps had sent it to comfort me. The dream ended. I woke up and got on with the day. Later that afternoon, when the kids came home from school, Josh announced that he had a present for me. Little boys *always* bring their moms presents: pictures they've drawn, work from school, bugs, snakes . . . But this one, Josh said, was special. He dug in his pocket with his dirty little hand. He dug and dug until, finally, he brought out one single red leaf.

Now I know for sure that Gramps is still watching, loving, and protecting me. As for Josh—well, he knew all along. ❀

—KELLY MCCLELLAND

Times were bad in Israel; the economy was struggling. It was difficult for anyone—the credentialed and the unskilled alike—to get a job. All over the country people were out of work, and housewives turned frugal and penny-pinching.

In this climate, Henya Lerman knew that she was indeed lucky to have found employment at a stable and well-respected company in Ramat Gan, a suburb of Tel Aviv. Henya considered herself not only fortunate, but blessed: The man who owned the company was an Orthodox Jew named Heshy Fleisher who was very sensitive to his employees' needs. Still, Henya couldn't help but worry: She was pregnant, due in three months, and wondered: *Will the boss grant me maternity leave and keep my job open until I'm ready to return to work?* Various scenarios played out in her head, and she fretted about the possibilities that loomed before her. Her husband had been out of work for over six months, and her brother, who lived with them, was also unemployed. Right now, she was the sole breadwinner of the family of three—soon to be four. The emotional burden was enormous.

Even at the annual company dinner—a lavish event that Mr. Fleisher arranged each year to honor and thank his employees—Henya couldn't stop agonizing. During a lull in the conversation, she began confiding her concerns to her colleagues. They cast warning glances in the boss's direction, but Mr. Fleisher's presence at the table didn't seem to dampen her volubility. Her coworkers began to shift uncomfortably in their seats, embarrassed at Henya's indiscretion. Perhaps she was desperately seeking their reassurance—or Mr. Fleisher's—but she certainly seemed to have blundered into a major faux pas. It was not a conversation fit for such a public venue.

Mr. Fleisher, however, was not as discomfited as his staff. He regarded Henya not with annoyance but with compassion, and carefully switched the topic. "Now that we're all here together," he said in a warm and friendly manner, "we have the rare opportunity to really get to know each other. We are, thank God, so busy at work we never have time to talk. I feel bad that I know so little personal information about my own staff. Where is everybody from originally, anyway?"

The segue was anything but smooth, but everyone at the table was relieved to change topics. People began talking eagerly about their respective pasts, backgrounds, histories. Israel was a land of immigrants. Hardly anyone at the table was a *Sabra* (a native-born Israeli).

"And where are *you* from, Henya?" Mr. Fleisher asked encouragingly.

"Oh, East Flatbush, Brooklyn," she answered shyly, still mortified by her blunder. "It was once a thriving section of Brooklyn but it's deteriorated into a very bad neighborhood now. None of my childhood friends live there anymore."

While Mr. Fleisher had been responsive to all of his employees' stories, it was Henya's reply that seemed to strike a chord. He began to bombard her with a series of rapid-fire questions: "Where exactly did you live in East Flatbush, Henya? When did you live there? What were your parents' names? Are they still alive? What *shul* (synagogue) did they attend?"

Mr. Fleisher could barely contain his excitement; Henya could barely conceal her surprise. The staff members kept looking back and forth at the two of them in bewilderment. Their confusion was compounded by the fact that Mr. Fleisher's eyes had begun to well with tears as he suddenly stood up and excused himself from the room. When he returned, his eyes were red-rimmed and he appeared overcome by emotion. He turned to Henya and said, "I want to tell you a story. Many years ago, two electricians lived in the old Jewish neighborhood of East Flatbush. One of them was a member of the Electricians' Union and very successful; the other one had been unable to join the union and was having a difficult time earning a decent wage. He was reduced to doing odd jobs that brought in very little money. Despite the differences in their lifestyles, the two became close friends. They *davened* (prayed) in the same shul, and often walked home together. They promised they would introduce their families to one another, but somehow they never did.

"One day, the poor electrician was suddenly stricken with a heart attack, and after a few days of touch-and-go, he died. When the wealthy electrician came to pay the family a *shiva* (condolence) call, he observed with sadness the destitute surroundings in which his friend had lived: the meager furniture, the scanty possessions, the frayed couch. He gently asked the widow if she had enough food at home for herself and her children and she quickly said, 'Yes.' But when he went into the kitchen, he inspected the cupboards and refrigerator and saw that both were bare. So, every single night during the seven-day period of the *shiva*, when the house was full of visitors and the widow was distracted, the electrician would sneak into the kitchen and stock the empty shelves with food.

"Two months later, the widow called the electrician and told him that her basement was full of all kinds of electrical supplies that her husband had used, and that she would like to sell him its entire contents for $100. The electrician promised he would come over that night to take a look, and he was dumbfounded at the sheer quantity of what his friend had amassed over the years. Much of it he deemed worthless, but scattered among the paraphernalia that littered the basement floor seemed to be a few items of value. The electrician told the widow that he would need some time to sort through the collection and assess its worth. For three weeks, the electrician came nightly and labored for hours in the basement, sorting through piles and heaps and layers of equipment, tools, and machinery, separating the junk from the surprising treasures, and organizing them into categories that only made sense to other members of his trade. Unbeknownst to the widow, the electrician had absolutely no intention whatsoever of paying her the $100 that she had requested and then taking off with the stuff. In his mind, he had engineered an entirely different plan of his own.

"When he had finished his massive undertaking, the electrician called all the contractors, builders, and jobbers that he knew and told them that he was conducting a sale on the following Sunday of various electrical supplies that they could use in their work. The sale was enormously successful, bringing in more than $3,000—a princely sum in those days. Needless to say, the electrician did not take the money for himself, but instead handed it over to the widow and her kids. This revenue helped sustain the family and keep them afloat for many months to come."

Mr. Fleisher ended the story with a heartfelt sigh and turned to Henya Lerman.

"Now let me introduce the cast of characters in this story. The incredibly kind electrician . . . that was your grandfather. The young orphans . . . one of them was *me*.

For it was my father who passed away, and it was your grandfather who saved us. Your grandfather's righteousness and charity saved my family's life."

Mr. Fleisher continued emotionally: "Mrs. Lerman, you need never worry about *parnosa* (money) again. I promise you that you will always have a job in my company. And if your husband and brother will please be so kind as to come to my office tomorrow, I'll find them both jobs, too."

Later that night, Henya wrote a letter to her grandfather, still alive in America, in which she recounted the episode, ending: "Thank you, Grandfather. I am so proud to be your grandchild. You not only saved this man's family; you saved mine." ❀

*A*s a lifelong supporter of the military, I was thrilled when my daughter Lisa was appointed to the U.S. Naval Academy's Class of '94. Remembering how important mail call was to my dad (a World War II navy veteran) when he was in the military, I sent a steady stream of letters, cards, and care packages.

Then, during December of Lisa's last year at the academy, tragedy struck. A carload of midshipmen returning from the Army/Navy game was crushed when a rain-soaked, rotten willow tree crashed across the highway less than a mile from the academy. Three girls died. One of them was Lisa. There would be no more outgoing letters filled with news of home, no more care packages or cookies and candy to be shared with class-mates, no more jokes and cartoons to make a frazzled "mid" (midshipwoman) and her friends laugh. As a free-lance writer, I would continue to write, but my favorite assignment was over. I was no longer "mail mom."

Then, one evening, I saw a "Dear Abby" column in

the newspaper asking people to write to servicemen who were away from their families over the holidays. *If it were my daughter away from home at Christmas, I'd want someone to write to her,* I thought. And, since Lisa had planned on becoming a marine, I decided that's precisely whom I would write to.

I sat down and wrote a long, newsy letter introducing myself, my hometown, and my family in as entertaining a way as possible. I mentioned Lisa, her years at USNA, and her tragic death in passing, as part of what had made me who I was today. For a moment, I wondered if mentioning her was wise. I hoped that it wouldn't make the recipients sad, but I knew that I couldn't leave it out. Lisa, after all, was my main reason for writing these letters in the first place.

I addressed several envelopes "Any Serviceman, USMC." To make them stand out, I decorated them with rubber-stamped bears playing the Marine Corps Hymn on bugles. I stuck a copy of my letter in each envelope and dropped them into the mail. I didn't really expect any answers. I knew servicemen were notorious about mail. They always seemed to be able to find the time to read it, but seldom seemed to have the time to answer!

Unbeknownst to me, my letters ended up on the USS *Guam*, where two young marines, going through "Any Serviceman" mail separately, randomly chose envelopes to read during their lonely hours. One chose a letter whose return address was near his Michigan hometown. The other chose one that was decorated with bugle-playing bears. When they returned to the room they shared, they were surprised to discover that they'd chosen letters from the same woman.

As the two men began to simultaneously read what turned out to be the exact same letter, they were again taken by surprise. The letter they had randomly chosen from tens of thousands was from the mother of their late classmate, Lisa Winslow, USNA '94. They immediately wrote back to me, sharing memories of Lisa and telling me how much it had meant to them—so close to the anniversary of her death—to receive news that her family was well. As for me, what a blessing their letters were! They told me things I had never known about Lisa and shared favorite anecdotes. Above all, it was comforting for me to know that Lisa had not been forgotten.

Several years later, another classmate of Lisa's wrote that he, too, had received an "Any Serviceman" letter from me that Christmas.

My envelopes may have been addressed to "Any Serviceman," but God knew their names—and mine. ❀

—BETTY WINSLOW

On a February morning in 1997, in the reception room of an orphanage in South China, an excited group of American men and women stood, shifting nervously from foot to foot, sipping tea, and waiting. After more than a year of filling out paperwork, sitting through interviews, and repeatedly checking mailboxes and fax machines for the much anticipated official OK, these people were about to meet the babies they had dreamed of holding in their arms—in some cases, for many, many years.

After a few anxious minutes, several Chinese women, including the orphanage director, entered the room, each carrying a baby. One by one, they handed the infants to their new parents, and the room started to buzz with moms, dads, and babies crying; cameras flashing; and videotapes rolling.

At that moment, the men and women in that crowded reception room joined the thousands of American families who have adopted Chinese children orphaned because of China's strict population-control laws. And two of the women in that group of new parents would soon discover a deeper connection, a bond so strong that it would change the course of their lives.

Cheri, a preschool teacher, had traveled all the way from her home in Pacifica, a town of 40,000 in northern California. She had always figured that she would get married and have children someday. That didn't happen, but her urge to have a child persisted. So Cheri decided to adopt. "I wanted to be a mother," she says, "and I knew someone who had adopted from China. I looked into domestic adoption, but being single, I thought it would be more difficult. And something about the Chinese culture drew me."

Gayle, a manager at a computer company in the southern California town of Carlsbad, had similar reasons for wanting to become a mother. She also wanted a child but was not married, and she began to feel that time was flying by. "One thing led to another," Gayle explains. "I had friends who had adopted, and they had very positive experiences." She started exploring her options, and after much thought and prayer, she settled on international adoption. "I attended a panel discussion on adoption, and I was deeply touched by the words of a woman who spoke about the situation in China," she adds. Gayle found a supportive agency, and after some frustrating delays, she was on her way to becoming a mother.

Cheri and Gayle had spoken briefly on the bus to the orphanage, but it wasn't until after they returned with their girls to Guangzhou, the capital of the Guangdong province in southern China, that they really began to build a friendship.

Cheri, Gayle, and other families spent the following ten days in Guangzhou, completing the paperwork required by the Chinese and American governments before they could take their babies home. The two women often sat together at meals, sharing typical new-mom anxieties. "There was a lot to think about with a new seven-month-old: what to feed her, how to care for her," says Cheri, who named her daughter Madison. Gayle chose the name Rachel for her little girl, also seven months old, according to the sketchy information in the documents they had received from the orphanage.

Finally, they were ready to return home. Cheri, Gayle, and the babies shared the same plane back to the States. They barely had time to say goodbye at the Los Angeles airport as each rushed to make her connecting flight home. But despite the long distance, the relationship between the two new families continued to grow.

"We began writing and sending pictures," Cheri says. "And we talked about getting together." More than a year had passed, though, when the mothers and daughters finally saw one another again.

The following May, Cheri, Madison, and Cheri's mother, Barbara, all flew down from San Francisco to visit Gayle, Rachel, and Gayle's mother, Jean. "As we approached Gayle's house, we heard voices coming from an outdoor patio, and the child's voice sounded a great deal like

Madison's," Cheri says. "We peeked into the patio and saw Rachel. It was like looking at Madison's double. We went inside and just kept staring at the girls side by side."

Back at the Chinese orphanage, when they first met their daughters, Cheri and Gayle had noticed similarities — and other parents in the group had commented on them as well. But the two new mothers didn't give them much thought. After all, the girls' paperwork reflected no tie between them. In fact, any link seemed impossible because, according to the papers, the babies had been found in two different places at two different times. "My mother, who had traveled with me to China, saw the similarities even more than I did," Gayle said. "I think I was still in a daze."

But now, at almost age two, the girls' resemblance was undeniable: Not only did they look alike, but their mannerisms and voices were identical. Anyone who saw them together came to the natural conclusion: They were twins.

After that weekend, Cheri says, "I felt that we needed to make sure we got together as often as we could." So when she began planning a family trip to Disneyland that fall, Cheri asked Gayle and Rachel to join them. While Madison and Rachel spun around in teacups and shook hands with Donald Duck, the two mothers discussed more weighty matters, such as whether to have DNA testing done on the girls to confirm the link.

Meanwhile, other tourists came up to them, asking if the girls were twins. "Gayle and I would look at each other and then say, 'We think so,'" Cheri remembers. But they wanted to know for certain: not just for their own benefit, but so that they would know what to say to the girls when they began asking questions themselves. "We wanted to be able to give them a definite answer," Cheri says.

In January 1999, each mother took a swab from inside her daughter's cheek and sent it for analysis to Affiliated Genetics, a DNA lab that Cheri had found on the Internet. After a six-week wait, the report came back: fraternal twins. The guesswork was over. "We just confirmed what we knew by then was true anyway," Cheri said.

That certainty changed everything: Though their lives had already been drifting together, Cheri and Gayle now knew they had an opportunity to give back to these girls the family they'd lost when they were abandoned by the Chinese birth parents. The timing couldn't have been better. Gayle was at a turning point in her career: Struggling to keep up with an increasingly demanding job while trying to raise her daughter, she was already looking for a more flexible position. Now that she knew for certain that Rachel and Madison were sisters, the idea of raising them together made perfect sense. She decided that she and Rachel would move north so that the two families would be closer to each other.

Although there were no job opportunities for Gayle in Pacifica, she found an area she loved just an hour away, in Petaluma. "Once the decision was made, every-thing just fell into place," she says. "My condo sold in a week. Rachel and I found a charming house to rent in three days. And 'Auntie Cheri,' Madison, and Cheri's parents came to visit our first weekend there."

The sisters have seen each other regularly since it was confirmed that they are family. "Their relationship is very sisterly, complete with sibling spats," Gayle says. "Each girl is growing into her own individual person and has a sister to share that with."

They also have an extended family through the two mothers. Even the grandparents are part of this very nontraditional union. "The two families that have been brought together by these little girls are so blessed by their strong connection," says Gayle's mother, Jean, who carries pictures of both Rachel and Madison in her wallet. "The sense of family is so strong, there are no boundaries here. Madison's mother and her grandparents have become part of my family." Although it would mean leaving many friends behind, Jean is also considering an eventual move from Santa Barbara to Petaluma. "I want to be closer to my two granddaughters and watch their progress in this adventure."

Cheri and Gayle share some of the parenting duties and have worked to synchronize their styles of communication. "We are, in essence, the two parents here," Cheri says. "We decided that what we say should be consistent." So they often talk about ways to handle the challenges of raising the girls. "Gayle and I are going to have to continue to talk and come up with answers together," Cheri says. "The girls started kindergarten this past

September, which will bring about a new set of questions—both about having a twin sister and not living with her, as well as the whole adoption issue."

Will they tell the girls how they came to be separated in the first place? "We've talked about 'birth father' and 'birth mother' with them," Gayle says, "and we've explained that they were together in their birth mother's tummy. We hope that growing up and spending time together might soften it for them. They will know that, as sisters, they'll always have each other."

Explaining how they were reunited, though, is simple, Cheri says. "I think it was fate. Gayle and I originally were scheduled to go to China at different times. And this probably wouldn't have worked as well if one child had been adopted by a couple and another by a single mother." Gayle believes fate played a role, too. "Rachel's Chinese name, Xiao Hui, means 'little reunion.' It's like someone knew the girls would find each other one day," she says.

Last summer, the twins celebrated their fifth birthday—together. In separate conversations, each girl, unbeknownst to the other, told her mother what she wanted for the party: a piñata. And so, amid fluttering crepe paper and a shower of sweets, Madison and Rachel blew out their candles as their mothers counted their blessings—times two. ❀

—KARIN EVANS

Reprinted with permission from *Health Magazine*, December 2001, page 76.

*I*saac* was beautiful on the inside—kind, sensitive, and considerate—but he did not project the kind of outer image that usually attracts women. His grooming and his social skills were . . . unpolished. At thirty years old, Isaac desperately wanted to get married. As an abandoned baby who had been adopted by a Jewish couple, Isaac had moved to Israel several years before. He made a meager living as an artist and lived in a small room in Jerusalem with a menagerie of other people's unwanted pets.

One day, Isaac decided to take a bold step. He placed a classified ad in the "Personals" section of *The Jerusalem Post*. It read: "Single Jewish male, vegetarian, animal lover, artistic, seeks wife for procreation."

Not surprisingly, no women responded.

Among the many *Post* readers who snickered at Isaac's ad and kept on reading was Marci.* Marci was twenty-nine years old, divorced, with two children. She had recently moved from America to a town in central Israel. Although Marci was gorgeous, she had one glaring drawback as a prospective wife: She had suffered a bout with cancer and was presently in remission. Marci was eager to remarry, especially to provide her children with a father. Combing the "Personals" in the *Post*, Marci found an ad that seemed promising:

"Single Jewish male, financially independent, educated, personable, seeks wife."

Marci called the number and made contact with Benson,* the writer of this second ad. They met the following night, and a whirlwind courtship ensued. But it did not lead to marriage. At the end of a few weeks, it was clear to Marci that Benson had no intention of getting married. He was looking for a good time, not a wife.

A short while after their breakup, Marci again perused the *Post*'s personals. To her horror, there was Benson's ad, again misleading unknowing women with its offer of marriage. Marci decided to play a little trick on him. From her new cell phone, she dialed his number, and in a false, alluring voice, left a tantalizing message on his voice mail.

Benson responded as soon as he heard the message, and a rendezvous was set up for that very night. But his mystery woman never showed up. After standing on the designated corner for half an hour in the rain, Benson called her number, only to discover a laughing Marci. He had been tricked.

Benson decided that he would have the last laugh. He bought the *Post* and searched the "Personals" for the most pathetic ad he could find, which was, of course, Isaac's "seeks wife for procreation" ad. He dialed the number, and when Isaac's voice mail answered, he played into it the alluring message Marci had left on his own voice mail, complete with her telephone number.

Isaac came home that day and pressed "Play" on his answering machine. To his surprise and happiness, someone had finally answered his long-running ad. He dialed her number right away.

Marci answered her phone. "Hello, I'm the one you called in response to my *Jerusalem Post* ad. My name is Isaac."

Marci was confused. "*I* called in response to your ad?"

"Yes," Isaac went on enthusiastically. "You said you wanted to meet as soon as possible, even tonight. I'm available tonight. Where do you want to meet?"

"B-b-but I didn't call you," Marci stammered.

"Yes, you did," Isaac insisted. "You left a message on my answering machine. I'll even play it for you."

As soon as Marci heard her steamy message, she understood what Benson had done. But now here was this poor fellow caught between her joke on Benson and his joke on her.

"So what time and where do you want to meet?" Isaac persisted, like a man who had never had a date before.

Marci hesitated. Why should this poor fellow suffer from her joke? Her kind heart got the better of her, and she acquiesced. "OK, I'll meet you tonight at eight."

Now, two years later, Isaac and Marci are married, with a one-year-old baby. Despite their striking outward differences, they actually have many things in common. Like Isaac, Marci is a vegetarian and an animal lover. And like Isaac, she was also an abandoned baby adopted by a Jewish couple.

No one who knew either one of them would ever have thought that the pair was a match. But thanks to a practical joke played on Marci by a roving-eyed Lothario, a date with destiny led to a walk down the aisle — proving once again that real life is always stranger than fiction! ❀

—Sora Rigler

*W*hy is it that the one thing you want most is sometimes the one thing you have to work the hardest for? Why does it seem as if some people have it all, while others feel forgotten by God? And why does what originally appeared to be a mere coincidence sometimes turn out to be the largest miracle of all? My friends Claire* and Bernie* grappled with these questions firsthand during a wrenching period in their lives.

Claire and Bernie had been married for six years and desperately wanted to start a family. Most of Claire's friends were already expecting their second child, but Claire had yet to conceive her first. Hearing her friends talk about "my baby this" and "my baby that" was almost too much to bear. Claire tried hard to maintain the high moral ground and not be petty, but sometimes she couldn't help but feel that life . . . or God . . . had been unfair. Her family began to make discreet suggestions that she make the rounds of fertility doctors, but Claire just couldn't bring herself to make the calls.

Claire often helped her husband Bernie in the charitable work he performed on a volunteer basis. Bernie spent a lot of his free time soliciting donations for various worthy organizations, and Claire assisted him in making "cold calls" to raise the money. One day, Bernie asked Claire to find the phone number for and call Mitch Delano,* an individual known for his generosity and dedication to philanthropic causes. Claire dialed operator assistance, obtained the number without difficulty, and was soon explaining the reason for her call to the woman who answered the phone. Claire quickly found out that she had not been given the phone number for Mitch Delano as she had requested, but for his brother, Dr. Harold Delano. The receptionist who had fielded the call proudly told her that Dr. Delano was one of the best-known and most successful fertility doctors in New York! Claire felt goose bumps travel up and down her arms. Was this a coincidence? Without thinking or first consulting with her husband, Claire impulsively made an appointment to see the doctor whose number she had dialed by mistake.

After the initial consultation and numerous tests, Claire and Bernie were sitting in the waiting room waiting to speak with the doctor. Claire thought that taking the tests had been difficult, but just sitting in the room gave the word *waiting* a whole new meaning. How could she pretend to be calm and read expired magazines in a waiting room when her whole future hung in the balance?

Finally, after what seemed like an eternity, the nurse

called Claire and Bernie into the doctor's office. Claire was trembling inside, whispering to herself, *Let him tell me good news, please.*

Dr. Delano was kind and compassionate, knowing how much hope his patients pinned on him. When Dr. Delano reviewed the test results with them, it wasn't what Claire wanted to hear. A childhood illness, which had seemed totally innocuous at the time, had damaged vital reproductive organs that were needed to bring a healthy pregnancy to fruition. Claire couldn't contain her anguish anymore and started crying. Bernie tried to comfort her, but inside he himself was breaking apart.

Dr. Delano allowed them the time to cry, and then asked them to give him a chance to finish his prognosis. Both tried to pull themselves together, threw their tissues in the garbage, took out some fresh ones, and held their breath.

"I myself am not Jewish," said Dr. Delano, "but I've had many Jewish couples come to my practice. Yes, your problem is physical, but not hopeless. While I wouldn't recommend surgery to correct what happened, because it will only cause further damage, I have learnt and witnessed the power of prayer. Your God is a compassionate God. I have seen it for myself. Miracles can occur when, according to x-rays, tests, and other modern medical methods, a prognosis seems to point to one definite negative conclusion."

Claire and Bernie did not know what to say. Just

walk out and pray? That was it? It seemed too easy! All this time, Claire's stance toward God had been in more of a complaining mode, the *why me?* stance. Now, she actually felt embarrassed to go back to God and beseech him to help her obtain her miracle. Would God forgive her for being so disrespectful and for always thinking of him in anger and petulance?

Claire's grandfather was a very learned man who daily made time for prayer and psalms. He always proclaimed his fervent belief that God is always there, always available. "All you have to do is knock on his door," her grandfather said.

Then and there, Claire decided to change her approach and attitude toward God. He truly was present in her life. The proof was having Dr. Delano tell her point-blank to pray! As if Dr. Delano himself was God's own messenger. But maybe he was, she reconsidered, thinking back to how she had come to find Dr. Delano in the first place.

Claire stood up, instilled with a new sense of purpose. She and her husband thanked Dr. Delano and promised to keep in touch. She practically skipped out of the office, Bernie trailing after her in puzzlement, not understanding her sudden change in behavior. They had been told that their chance to start a family was practically one in a million and Claire was happy?

As they were walking to the car, Claire explained: "For the first time, we've been given a chance. For the first time, I understand what my grandfather told us when we were children. I wish I had paid more attention to his words then. God *wants* us to turn to him. Yes, he's placed modern technology at our fingertips, but it is to him that we must turn first, last, and always. I feel that a lamp has finally illuminated my life, and now I know that whatever the outcome, God is here with us. Our prayers are heard. Even if the answer is sometimes 'No.'"

Bernie felt enlightened and encouraged by his wife's words. He too realized that he had been remiss and lacking in his faith.

Three years later, Claire and Bernie found themselves back in Dr. Delano's office once again.

"Congratulations," Dr. Delano beamed. "You're just about three months pregnant."

Once again, Claire cried in his office, ecstatic, not quite believing the news.

Dr. Delano continued, "Yes, you are pregnant, but you have to be very careful; we will have to watch you and pretty much keep you on bed rest."

But Claire was too overjoyed to have her spirits dampened by Dr. Delano's cautionary words. What mattered most was the word "Yes" that had come from God after he had heard her prayers.

Then and there Claire began to map out how she and her husband would raise their child. One thing was certain: She would never let the child forget that prayer has the strength to change *any* decree. ❀

—ELKY FAIVISH

*N*o one knew that she had a weak heart. No one knew that giving birth would make it weaker. Her circumstances were dire, for she lived in great poverty with a husband who was largely absent and indifferent. The first time she gave birth to a son, her heart faltered. The second time around—a son again—she could barely breathe.

No one remembers exactly who it was who decided to tell her falsely that the second child had been stillborn. Regardless of who made the decision, it was clear that she was physically and emotionally incapable of handling a second child. Whoever had made the decision to put the baby up for adoption did so out of regard for the lives of both mother and newborn. She was told that her baby was dead. She never learned the truth.

"Every Valentine's Day, my mother would cry and say, 'Dino, oh Dino!'" Mario Lussier, the first son, remembers. There were only three things he had been told about his younger brother: He had been born on February 14th, his mother had named him Dino, and he had died at birth.

In 1978, the young mother's heart gave out. She died never knowing that her second son was indeed well and alive, adopted into a loving family and renamed Robert.

Then the miracle occurred. The same weak heart that had been responsible for killing her and separating the two brothers brought them back together again.

Both sons apparently had inherited the same weak heart. But their circumstances, some twenty-odd years after their mother's, were vastly different. Time and technology were on their side; great medical strides had been made over the years in the treatment of heart failure; and both had insurance to cover the advanced procedures that would save their lives.

Like his mother before him, Mario Lussier was dying of cardiac failure. In the nick of time, he was sent to Royal Victoria Hospital in Montreal, where he underwent a successful heart transplant and was restored to life.

Five years later, another young man, stricken with the exact same problem, was on the same floor of the same hospital about to undergo the exact same procedure.

Simone Sirois, a nurse and coordinator of the organ transplant unit at Royal Victoria Hospital, met the new patient—whose name was Robert—and blinked. After interviewing him, she impulsively picked up the phone and dialed Mario Lussier, who had been under her care five years before. "I've just seen your double," she said.

Mario told her that it was impossible that he was related to her new patient. Although it was true that his mother had actually given birth to a second son, he had died during childbirth.

But the resemblance was too striking for Simone to shrug off.

"Do you remember when he was born?" Simone asked him.

"Valentine's Day," Mario answered promptly. "February 14th."

Simone checked the hospital records and learned that Robert's birth date was February 14th, too. *OK, it could be a weird coincidence,* she thought.

But something made "Miss Marple" press on. All transplant patients have to be tissue typed, so the hospital had samples for both Robert and Mario. After checking, Simone discovered that their tissue samples were *identical.* This proved conclusively that Mario and Robert were brothers and that Robert was in fact none other than Dino, long thought to be dead.

"If you saw this on the soaps, you'd think 'Yeah, sure,'" Simone said.

Because Dino/Robert was undergoing surgery the very next day, Simone and the hospital administrators decided it would be prudent to wait until he was out of intensive care before disclosing the astonishing news. They didn't want to give either of his hearts—the new one he was about to get or the old one he was about to discard—any untoward shocks.

When he was out of harm's way and the secret was

finally disclosed, Robert shook his head in disbelief. "To get a heart and a brother at the same time . . . that's a lot," he told the press when he and his brother held a news conference at the hospital.

The first meeting was momentous for both men. Mario visited Robert at the hospital. "I walked in, we looked at each other, and we couldn't move," Mario said.

"Robert's adoptive mother was there to witness the reunion, and she pushed me forward," Mario said. "We hugged and we cried. When we looked at each other, it was as if we were looking into a mirror."

Simone Sirois told reporters that it was a fluke that Robert had ended up in her ward at Royal Victoria Hospital.

"He had been treated at Sacre Coeur Hospital, and they typically send their patients to the Montreal Heart Institute for transplants rather than here," she explained. "But he got sick very suddenly, so his parents took him to Lakeshore Hospital, which then had him transported to us. It was just by chance that he ended up here, and something clicked inside my head when I saw him." ❀

$\mathcal{D}$o dead people talk?

Or, to put it another way, can the deceased make contact with loved ones who still reside on this earthly plane via signs, symbols, and dreams?

Charley Levine is one of the most highly regarded public relations professionals living in Israel. Director of the distinguished Ruder Finn PR Agency in Jerusalem, Charley is hardly the type to believe in ghosts. But one of the family treasures that he has inherited from his father Dan—a Texas businessman who was also a respected community leader—is an incredible story about his Grandpa Abie's heavenly communication to his dad. As Charley recounts it:

My dad, Dan Levine, was president of Rodfei Sholom Synagogue in San Antonio, Texas. One of the proudest moments in his life was the day that he and his father—Grandpa Abie—dedicated one of the beautiful new synagogue's huge stained glass windows, each of which depicted a different Jewish holy day. Only a short time later, Grandpa Abie passed away, on the eve of Yom Kippur—the holiest day of the year.

Because the holiest day of the year was only hours away, special mourning conditions applied. Rather than a funeral followed by the usual full week of prescribed mourning, the *shiva* period was dispensed with, in accordance with Jewish law. Thus, only hours after experiencing the shock of my grandfather's passing, my father found himself sitting, not on a low mourner's bench in the quiet of his family home, but rather, on the center stage of Rodfei Sholom, sitting in the synagogue's imposing high-backed president's seat.

Although he faced hundreds of friends, family, and congregants, my father felt terribly alone in his sorrow. The shock of the morning's events had begun to wear off, replaced by a deep, gnawing pain and heart-wrenching loneliness. As the inspiring *"Kol Nidre"* prayer was intoned and the services moved forward, my father's thoughts compulsively returned to his loss.

My mother's and siblings' eyes—in the rows facing him—shared his hurt and probed for signs that he was coping, but my father didn't return our anxious looks. His eyes closed instead as his thoughts turned skyward. Certain thoughts kept going through his mind and he could not cast them away. Finally, he whispered a little prayer: "Dad, I know I shouldn't bother you, but I have to know if you are all right. I'm not the kind of person who asks these questions usually, but is there any way . . . any way at all, that you can let me know I shouldn't worry? Dad, is it possible for you to give me a sign?"

The minutes dragged by as these obsessive thoughts commanded my grieving father's attention.

It was a dry, windless late summer night in San Antonio. No sweaters in sight. No rain boots in the outer foyer closet.

But that didn't keep the lightning from striking. First, a tremendous clap of thunder, accompanied— almost simultaneously—by the proverbial bolt of lightning. The congregation emitted a surprised collective gasp, and even the cantor stopped short for a moment. Everyone tensed and waited for more, assuming that this was the beginning of a freak storm, but that was it. No additional strokes of lightning brightened the skies; no further sounds of thunder rumbled through the night. It was as if the whole thing had never even happened.

Jolted from his deepest turmoil and pleadings, my father blinked in the light and his eyes were immediately drawn to the synagogue's stained glass window that he and his father had donated, and dedicated, just a few weeks before. There his gaze was riveted in shock.

A five-foot crack had suddenly appeared in the brand-new window, running down its surface, caused by the single dramatic stroke of lightning. Of all the stained glass windows in the synagogue, only my grandfather's was affected. Not a single other one showed so much as a scratch.

It took a moment for my father to absorb this fact, but not much more than that. He had begged for a sign on Yom Kippur, and his appeal had been answered in this graphically explicit and meaningful way.

As the story circulated that evening and for days and weeks to come in San Antonio, people focused on the spectacular character of what had happened. The message for my father, however, was quite different.

He didn't really care about the melodrama or the unusual split-second thunderstorm. All he really cared about was one thing—he had received the answer to his question: "Dad, are you all right?" ❀

—CHARLEY LEVINE

*H*e was crouched in a corner, covering his mouth with a wet, dirty rag, trying hard not to breathe in the acrid smell of sulfur that accompanied the Allied bombings. In the last months of World War II, he had gone underground, scurrying from one hiding place to another. He lived on instinct alone, his world suddenly consisting solely of tunnels, sewers, cellars, spaces sunk deep beneath the earth, far away from prying eyes and vindictive tongues. He was fifteen years old, a Jew and an orphan. His parents had perished in the camps, and his siblings were missing. In the places of concealment that he inhabited, he was always alone.

Now, however, he was sharing his hiding place—a cramped, rubble-strewn basement—with several strangers, who huddled together for safety. The bombs had begun pelting the streets minutes earlier, and he had slunk into the nearest refuge. He imagined that the others were ordinary German citizens seeking shelter from the bombardment. The town had been emptied of its Jewish population long before, although a few, like him, still dwelled in the shadowy netherworlds that had not yet been fully penetrated.

Sometimes, when the basic impulse for survival that propelled him faltered, he wondered why he continued to fight. His family was gone, his community had disappeared, life as he had known it had ceased to exist. What was the point? But the final words of his mother, as she was dragged away by the Nazis to the waiting cattle cars, still rang in his ears.

"Leibel," she had shouted, "don't give up. Fight! You will be the remnant."

And then, as the soldiers hauled her away, she shouted one last time: "I will help you!"

He shuddered as he remembered the scene. It was inconceivable to him that she was gone. She had always been such a strong, vital presence, such a source of comfort and strength. How could she have disappeared into mere ash? He held her image in front of his eyes and made her alive again in his imagination.

He thought of his mother now—even as the bombs fell—crying inside his soul, a teenager trying to be a man: *How long, Mama? I don't know how much more I can hold out. I love you, Mama. I miss you.*

Just then, as if in answer to his reveries, a soft, gentle, familiar voice began to call his name. "*Leibela*," it whispered. It had been his mother's term of endearment for him. "*Leibel*."

Was he finally losing his mind? He turned to look at

the strangers crouched next to him. Had they too heard? Had they too heard his beloved mother's unmistakably clear and melodious voice?

No one rustled, no one stirred. Even in the gloom, he could see their expressions unchanging, registering nothing.

But now he heard it again, strong and insistent.

Was this someone playing a joke? But how could that be? The streets were desolate and empty, the frightened citizenry hiding from the bombs. Who would dare venture outside now? And who could possibly know his name?

But there it was again—the pure, sweet voice that stirred his soul, the soul he thought already dead.

"Leibel, Leibela . . ."

The voice was coming from outside the shuttered basement window, beckoning him to the street. It was at once hypnotic and commanding. Perhaps his mother had survived and miraculously found her way to him? He had to know. Leibel straightened his legs, sprang up from his crouched position, and pushed his way through the densely packed bodies toward the basement door.

"Hey," shouted one stooped figure in disbelief, grabbing his arm as he passed. "The all-clear hasn't sounded yet. The bombs are still coming down. You can't go out yet. It's not safe."

"My mother's there," Leibel said. "I hear her calling me. I've got to get to my mother."

"You're crazy," the man said. "No one's out there."

"Listen, I hear her now," Leibel cried. "Don't you hear that voice?"

"*Leibel, Leibela.*" First it had been a caress, then a soft beckoning. Now it had become a summons.

"I hear nothing," the man said. "You're hallucinating."

"I have to find my mother!" Leibel shouted, shoving the man out of his path and ascending the ladder to the street above.

It was desolate, eerily quiet, and utterly deserted. No figure of any kind—male or female—hovered nearby. Yet still he heard the voice, pulling him away from the quarters in which he had encamped, farther down the street. He blindly followed the voice, desperate to find its source.

Suddenly, a bomb exploded in the distance. Smoke spiraled out of the makeshift bomb shelter where he had been hiding. He heard the screams coming from the basement and stood frozen in shock, stunned at the fate of the company of men he had just left, but awed at the miracle that had snatched him from the jaws of death.

"*Leibel, Leibela . . .*" He strained to hear the beloved voice once more, but it had abruptly faded and was gone.

Throughout his childhood, this had been the voice that lulled him to sleep, hushed his cries, soothed his imaginary hurts, eased his fears, and offered compassion, solace, and strength. The voice had been neither muted nor stilled by death. From beyond the grave—far beyond this world—it had reached out to Leibel, and, mysteriously but inexorably, saved his life. ✿

*I*t's hard to know when to bless the light and curse the darkness. That's because life so often takes us by surprise. Strange reversals, twists of fate, surprise endings. These things are the stuff of real life, not just fiction. Frequently, a situation that we were so sure was a blessing develops—either suddenly or very slowly—into a veritable curse that we pray will disappear. And the exact opposite holds true as well. Sometimes, the very same set of circumstances that we originally deemed to be a great misfortune turns out to be a gift from God instead. This was precisely the state of affairs that Jean Irish of Welland, Ontario, experienced several years ago.

In the spring of 1997, Jean came home one afternoon and was fumbling with her keys when she noticed that her front door was ajar. Inside, she found her apartment ransacked and all her valuables stolen: her TV, stereo, and several hundred dollars in cash. She felt shaky, vulnerable, and sad. *It's all so senseless,* she thought. Jean liked to place optimistic spins on mishaps and mistakes, but what possible good could come out of a robbery?

Meanwhile, across the city, Martha Chernis was particularly riveted by an article in the local newspaper recounting the burglary. Robberies—even in smaller, quieter cities such as Welland—aren't uncommon events, and Martha would have quickly skimmed the story and moved on, had it not been for one minor detail: the name of the robbery victim. To see that name in print paralyzed the young reader, because it belonged to the very woman she had been seeking for years—her biological mother, Jean Irish.

Martha tried to maintain her calm, but, in fact, she was stunned. "Mom," she asked her adoptive mother Marie Vollick as she pointed out the newspaper story, "do you think it could be her? I'm scared to ask."

"I'll call," Marie quickly offered. "If we don't try, we'll never know." When Marie couldn't obtain Jean Irish's number through the usual channels, she turned to the local police, who were able to provide the number for her.

"You don't know me," Marie told Jean gently when she answered the phone. "But I believe we may have adopted your biological daughter."

"But how can that be?" Jean's voice trembled in shock. "Years ago, when I tried to find her, I was told by a search agency that she had been killed in a car crash! . . . What was her birth name?" Jean probed cautiously, seeking confirmation.

"Susan Anne!" Marie cried.

"Oh, my God. How did you find me after all these

years?" Jean asked.

When Marie recounted the sequence of events that had led to this moment, Jean felt goose bumps break out all over her body. The robbery had seemed so senseless before, but now it was beginning to take on deeper, more profound dimensions. It was going to serve as the poignant catalyst for a mother and child reunion.

That night, Jean and Marie kissed and hugged in a tearful and moving encounter.

"I must be the only person alive who considers herself lucky to have been robbed," Jean said. ❀

*T*here are always expectations when families gather round for holiday festivities. These expectations range from the more mundane—lavishly set tables groaning under the weight of wonderful food, the exchange of extravagant gifts—to the more sublime—the sense of spiritual significance and the link to one's history and heritage. No matter what religious tradition one belongs to, holidays are about hope, belief, and expectation.

The first night of Chanukah in the winter of 1980 was no different from any other Chanukuh as the extended Levin* clan assembled in the family room to light the menorah candles perched on the window ledge. As always, the atmosphere was thick with the varied expectations of both young and old: The children stole sidelong, impatient glances at the gift-wrapped packages heaped in a pile on the floor, while the men peeked with anticipation at the steaming platters of food. Eyes glinted with excitement as the patriarch of the family bent to light the first candle, and the night began to unfold.

Then the unexpected happened—a sudden and unforeseen deviation from the timeless script. As the mother raised the window shade so that the menorah could be lit in full view of the street, the children began to giggle and point. For there, perched on the other side of the window, shivering in the cold and tapping the pane with its beak, was a big, beautiful parrot!

"What is a parrot doing outside in the dead of winter in Brooklyn?" sputtered one uncle as pandemonium erupted.

"It must have escaped from its home!" screamed an excited child.

"It looks so cold," cried another youngster. "Can't we let it in?"

Mothers raised their eyebrows dubiously; fathers shrugged their shoulders, at a loss as to what to do. But the children clamored long and hard for the poor parrot to be let in.

"Look, Mom," suggested a ten-year-old persuader, already a shoo-in for the legal profession. "Why don't we let it in now to keep it warm and safe, and tomorrow, we'll canvass the neighborhood and find its owner? If it stays outside, it might die!"

The mothers pitied the parrot, clearly out of its element and freezing in the cold. The window was opened, the bird burst into the room, and the youngsters squealed in delight, as the parrot flew around in circles flapping its wings. Finally, the ten-year-old caught the parrot, placed it in an old unused hamster cage, and gave it some food. After the brouhaha subsided, the patriarch returned to the menorah and the rest of the evening proceeded as planned.

The next morning, the Levin kids dutifully began making the rounds of the neighborhood. They were sure they would find the rightful owner quickly, surmising that the parrot couldn't have strayed far from its home — but after hours of knocking on doors, they came up empty. Not only hadn't anyone lost a parrot, no one even *knew* anyone who owned one. "Does the parrot say anything?" one man asked. "Maybe you'll find a clue there."

"Oh, that's a great idea," Benjy, the ten-year-old pre-law student agreed. "Maybe it'll say the name of its owner!"

"That would indeed be helpful," the man acknowledged with a wry grin.

The kids ran back home to ask their mother if the parrot had said anything during their absence that would provide them with a significant lead.

"I don't know what the average vocabulary of your average parrot is," their mother said, "but this parrot just keeps on repeating one phrase and one phrase only. In *Yiddish* of all things."

"What does it say?" the kids squealed.

"Tzipporah, gey shloffen!" ("Tzipporah, go to sleep!")

"Well, at least we know it's a Jewish bird," joked Miriam, the twelve-year-old.

"Wow, that's great, Mom!" enthused Benjy. "We just

have to find someone named Tzipporah. That should be easy enough." The would-be Hardy Boys and Nancy Drews turned on their heels and returned to the streets to canvass the neighbors again. But once more, their quest proved futile. None of the neighbors knew any one named Tzipporah and no one was missing a parrot.

"Let's put up some posters!" Bruce, the eldest of the siblings, suggested. So they plastered the neighborhood with posters. Later, they tried leaving fliers on everyone's doorstep. They even reported their find to the local police station. But despite all their attempts, the owner of the parrot could not be found.

"So can we keep it, Mom?" the Levin kids pressed.

"I guess so," she smiled. "You've done your best to find the owner, and I suppose, by default, the parrot belongs to you now."

The Levin kids named their new parrot Miracle, because they had found it (or rather the parrot had found *them*) on the first night of Chanukah, a holiday about miracles.

Years later, the kids were grown-up—some had moved out of the house, a few had married—but Miracle the parrot was still safely ensconced in the Levin household. Benjy was now nineteen, and dorming in a college near Boston. Chanukah and Christmas usually more or less coincided on the calendar, but this year Chanukah was earlier, and Christmas vacation was still two weeks away. Benjy couldn't miss finals, so he had no choice but to remain in school. For the first time in his life, Benjy found himself without family on Chanukah, and he felt very much alone. So he decided to check out the university's chapter of Hillel—a club for Jewish students—which had advertised a Chanukah party in the school newspaper.

There were about 200 students in the dining room, which contained a huge menorah. *Latkes* (Chanukah pancakes) and *sufganiyot* (Chanukah doughnuts) filled the air with their tantalizing aromas. Benjy sniffed the familiar scents happily, and his spirits soared. Later—after the menorah had been lit, the blessings recited, the melodies sung, and the food consumed—kids sat on the floor in a big circle and, prompted by the Hillel rabbi, talked about the meaning of miracles and Chanukah. First, the talk was serious and spiritual, but as the night wore on, conversation turned more lighthearted and funny. It was at this juncture that Benjy volunteered his "Miracle the Parrot" story, a tried-and-tested anecdote that never failed to elicit chuckles and good cheer.

Benjy had just finished the well-worn line that was always good for a few laughs . . . "But the only words that the parrot ever said were *'Tzipporah, gey shloffen!'*" . . . when he noticed a young woman staring at him intently. He had noticed her before, but had been afraid to approach her because she was intimidatingly beautiful. She, in turn, had appeared oblivious of him. But now, yes, she was definitely *staring* at him, and he wondered if he had made a complete idiot of himself by recounting the story. Maybe it was too juvenile? Maybe it was time for him to retire it from his repertoire?

After the circle broke up, she approached him. "Excuse me," she said, "but I think you have my parrot. You see . . . *I'm Tzipporah!*"

This *could* have been the beginning of the fiercest of conflicts and clashes over the aging parrot, but thankfully, the case never had to be tried in the rabbinical courts. For, as Benjy and Tzipporah began first to laugh, then to argue, and then to laugh all over again about whom Miracle belonged to, a miracle of its own was in the making—the miracle of love. Benjy and Tzipporah went out for coffee to argue their respective sides, discovered they had a lot in common besides the parrot, fell in love, decided to get married, and took custody of Miracle *together*! It was a Chanukah miracle, all right, because they might never have met if it hadn't been for their many-feathered friend!

Benjy and Tzipporah are about to celebrate their tenth Chanukah together as a couple, the only sad note in their lives so far being the departure of Miracle to the great parrot heaven in the sky.

So now, it's Benjy who urges his wife at the end of a long and happy day: "*Tzipporah, gey shloffen.*" And smiling tenderly at her beloved, who never forgets the phrase that first brought them together, she falls asleep. ❈

For many years, my husband Mark and I lived in an old-fashioned farmhouse with our children, Lisa, Michael, Matthew, and Amanda. As the children grew, we took a lot of pictures of them. Often, we had them pose standing next to a certain bush in our yard. The bush started out small, but like our kids, grew tall. Over the course of time, the bush blossomed into a wonderful backdrop, and, depending on the season, was alternately covered with sweetly scented flowers, bright green leaves, or piles of sparkling snow. As avid gardeners, we knew it was officially called a "mock orange bush," but to us, it was simply "the Bush," and pictures taken in front of it were labeled "Bush Pictures."

Lots of family history occurred in front of the Bush: Matt and Amanda laughing during an Easter egg hunt; the kids nervously clutching backpacks on their first day of school; Mike mugging for the camera before his first school dance; Lisa beaming with pride on her first leave home from the Naval Academy.

When Lisa died in a freak car accident a few months short of her USNA graduation, the walls of the funeral parlor were covered with pictures of her. The "Bush Pictures" brought tearful smiles as we remembered asking her to pose yet again. "Oh, Mom, do I have to? Come on!" she'd moan. "Yes, you do!" I'd insist. Then, grinning and striking a pose, she'd sling an arm around the nearest sibling and oblige me all over again.

After her death, when her friends came to visit and exchange "Lisa stories," we wanted them to be able to stay with us, but the farmhouse just wasn't big enough. After several years and a lot of thought, we decided to move into a larger house in town. I knew that leaving the farmhouse would be hard, but to my surprise, the hardest part was leaving "the Bush." It had marked the seasons and the changes in my children as they posed in front of it. How I wished I could take it with us!

At the new house, I decided to plant a memorial garden to ensure that Lisa's presence—at least in spirit—would remain an integral part of our surroundings. I selected the flowers I wanted to plant carefully; they were flowers that "spoke" of my memories of Lisa in old-fashioned flower language. Although the yard was mired in the dregs of winter, I poked around a little and found, at the end of a neatly pruned hedge, a spot that looked exactly right for what I had in mind—except for the bush right next to it. Since this bush was bare, a bit scraggly, and obviously not part of the main hedge, we thought it might need to go.

But I would wait until spring to decide its fate.

Meanwhile, as I impatiently waited for spring's arrival, I drew up a list of our family's favorite flowers and also researched the meanings that each flower had held over the years. Scarlet poppies—Mark's favorite— meant "consolation," while marigolds, grown everywhere we'd ever lived, meant "grief." Pansies, one of my own personal favorites, said "you occupy my thoughts," while lilies of the valley meant "return of happiness." As I continued to read about the significance of different plants and flowers, I was delighted to stumble across an entry for the mock orange bush. Mock orange, I read, meant "remembrance." As I looked at Lisa's "Bush Pictures" that graced the walls of the new house, it seemed magically appropriate, and I mourned anew for the bush that had sheltered so many family memories.

When spring finally arrived, unsuspected treasures bloomed everywhere. Crocuses peeked through the snow by the front door, sunshine daffodils waved along the fence, and violets painted the sideyards royal purple. I would have stepped outside more often to see what new plants and flowers had blossomed overnight, but I was in the house constantly, trying to get it into shape. Settling into a new house is a lot of work, so I was basically content to leave the yard to Mark's attentions.

One week I was on a particular roll, spending several days in a whirlwind of unpacking cartons and boxes. I was so consumed and obsessed by my work that during this period I hadn't even looked out the window once. Mark stopped me one day and insisted, "You have to get out. Come with me; there's something I want to show you!" Glad for an excuse to stop working—even for a few minutes—I followed him to the corner that I had set aside for Lisa's memorial garden.

There, spreading green leaves and fragrant blossoms over her spot, was the scraggly bush I had been so unsure of. I tipped my head back and looked up at its branches and smiled, tears in my eyes. It was a mock orange bush. Remembrance had been here, waiting for us, all along. ✤

—BETTY WINSLOW

*G*randma Harter always made me feel special.
Throughout my childhood and young adulthood, we had always had a close relationship and I loved her dearly. So when she gave me as a wedding gift a pair of linen pillowcases that she had sewn herself and embroidered with beautifully crocheted flowers, they were more meaningful to me than practically anything else I received. Whatever came from Grandma Harter's talented hands and loving heart would always be filled with sentiment and significance. After my wedding, I took pains to properly launder and care for the pillowcases. I treated those pillowcases with the same reverence with which someone else might handle fragile china.

When my husband, Gary, received a job offer to be the director of a hospital pharmacy in Ottumwa, Iowa, we became giddy with excitement. Between the two of us, we had been working four jobs and taking care of a newborn baby to boot. Now, we could settle down into a more stable life, and Gary would have an eight-to-five job with an actual paycheck! And, to top it all off, the move meant that we would be in much closer proximity to Grandma Harter, whose home was only a few miles north of Ottumwa. We couldn't have been more thrilled.

In the days building up to the big move, we began packing away our possessions in the boxes and cartons that littered our floor. I was particularly fastidious with the pillowcases, which I carefully wrapped with other bedding items.

Since we didn't have the money to hire commercial movers, Gary borrowed a big truck from a friend, who helped him carefully load all the boxes along with the few sparse pieces of furniture we owned. Because the skies were overcast and it looked like rain, a tarpaulin was tightly fastened over the load as we headed out for the two-hour trip to our new home. By mid-afternoon, we had unloaded the truck and were observing thankfully that all its contents had arrived intact—and dry.

There are no words to describe our reaction when Grandma appeared the very next morning as we began to put our old things into new places. We thought she had come to welcome us—which she had, but she also had something she needed to tell us. We gladly took a break and shared a pot of coffee as she began to recount her story.

She had been busy the day before, she told us, baking pies for the freezer all day. In fact, that's probably exactly what she was doing as our moving truck traveled past her farm on Highway 63 on the way to our destination.

Because she was consumed all day by her project, she neglected to check the mailbox until dusk. It was twilight by the time she finally made her way down the long path towards the mailbox, and she could barely see.

As Grandma approached the highway where the rural mail carrier made daily deliveries, she noticed something wrapped around the wooden post that held the metal box. Since she couldn't figure out what it was, she retrieved the object, together with the mail, and returned home. It wasn't until she got back into the house and made the discovery near the living room lamp that she gasped. She couldn't believe her eyes. She was holding a pillowcase very familiar to her—it revealed the delicate floral trim that she, herself, had crocheted on this crisp, white linen four years ago!

Now, sitting at our small kitchen table, Grandma Harter reached into her canvas bag, pulled out the pillowcase, and handed it to me. I knew that there had to be some kind of mistake, some explanation. I went to the hall closet, which contained the linen I had unpacked the previous night. Sure enough, there I found only *one* of Grandma's cherished pillowcases—half of her wedding gift. I hadn't noticed that one of the pillowcases was missing when I hurriedly removed the bedding from the cartons the night before. As I stood there, holding the reunited pair in my hands, the impact of this incident hit me.

What were the odds of this precious keepsake

landing at—of all places—Grandma's door, when we had probably passed hundreds of rural mailboxes as we traveled approximately 100 miles from Iowa City to Highway 63 in Ottumwa?

And how could this smooth linen fabric cling and remain attached to Grandma's mailbox all day long, on a day that was both windy and rainy? And perhaps the most inexplicable aspect of this story: How did this singular pillowcase end up with Grandma when all the boxes arrived at our new home still taped and intact—and nothing else was missing?

I'd always known that I had a special bond with this woman, a spiritual connection that remained unbroken over the decades, even following her death a few years later. But on that memorable June day when the three of us silently hugged each other in that tiny kitchen, I knew that there are some ties that transcend logical explanation and create miracles. ❀

—SHIRLEY JONES

*I*t was 1942. The Warsaw Ghetto—scene of the most heroic resistance effort by Jews during the nightmare years of the Holocaust—had not yet been liquidated. Stealthy figures crossed the streets when night fell, bringing food, forged documents, money, and guns into the beleaguered zone. Shadows huddled together in clandestine conversations, and quick handshakes sealed hastily negotiated transactions. On many of the deals that were made, human life hung in the balance.

Dr. Laibel Friedman*, one of the most prominent activists in the Warsaw Ghetto, and later one of its few survivors and foremost historians, often engaged in whispered exchanges. A member of the Warsaw Ghetto's Community Council and an outstanding leader, he was zealous about Jewish survival. Thirty-five years old, he was no longer as nimble as his teenage cohorts who navigated the sewers, tunnels, and bunkers. Yet in his own inimitable way, Laibel Friedman took grave risks, made enormous sacrifices, and compromised his personal security on a daily basis. A devoted champion of his people, Dr. Friedman did everything within his power to save Jewish lives.

One night, he was approached by a man who told him a heartbreaking story. A young child in the Ghetto, Miriam Brand,* had been orphaned. Both of her parents had been killed and there was no one left to care for her. Could Dr. Friedman use his connections to get her Aryan papers and smuggle her out of the Ghetto? Like all the urgent favors asked of him, this one posed serious risks. Being found out could have cost him his life. But he didn't hesitate for a fraction of a second. The suffering of his people never failed to touch a responsive chord within him, even when it placed him in peril. "Of course," he replied instantly. "I'll see what I can do."

Laibel Friedman never disappointed anyone; he was true to his word. The young girl was successfully smuggled out of the Ghetto, and the activists inside lost touch with those delivering her to safety. Dr. Friedman moved on to the next case. There was always something new and urgent to attend to. Meanwhile, the Ghetto became increasingly isolated and under siege; there was no way of tracking the orphan's movements or ascertaining her fate. Communication with the outside world was erratic and rare. Dr. Friedman had no idea where the little girl was, or even whether the child for whom he had risked so much was dead or alive.

Fast forward thirty-five years. Dr. Friedman, one of the Ghetto's few survivors, was now a distinguished author, a prolific journalist, and a respected historian. He had made a life for himself in Brooklyn, New York, and had sired a family of four brilliant and talented children. One of them, Mordechai,* was considered an *ilui* (genius) in Talmudic studies. The renowned *Rosh Yeshiva* (head of the rabbinical seminary in which the young man studied) cast his eye on him as a prospective mate for his own daughter. A matchmaker was called to serve as intermediary; the young couple were introduced and met many times; the match was made. Dr. Friedman was ecstatic. In the Orthodox Jewish community in which he lived, the match was considered stellar by any standard. To be chosen by the *Rosh Yeshiva* as a son-in-law was a spectacular achievement—a triumph, a cause for great joy and pride. It was an emblem of the highest affirmation of his son's standing in the community, and a harbinger of great things to come. Dr. Friedman was overwhelmed with gratitude to God.

On the eve of the engagement, before it was officially announced to the world at large, Dr. Friedman and his wife were invited to the home of the *Rosh Yeshiva* to meet the young bride and her parents. There he met the woman whom he had smuggled out of the Warsaw Ghetto as a young girl so many decades ago and who, indeed, was none other than his beloved son's future mother-in-law. ❀

When Benjamin "Bucky" Becker met Lillian "Lakey" Holcomb in Baltimore, Maryland, in 1936, he was nineteen years old and she was seventeen. Bucky was friends with Lakey's older brother and frequently came over to the Holcomb home to visit. It was inevitable that the two would eventually meet.

The first time they did meet, not a single word passed between the two. Lakey was sitting on a chair, reading a book in the living room, when Bucky sauntered in, looking for her brother. The two stared at one another for a long moment, speechless. Then Bucky turned around and left the room.

When Bucky reappeared the following week for another visit, he finally spoke up. This time, however, he forgot about his initial reason for being at the Holcomb home (ostensibly to visit her brother again) and asked Lakey if she wanted to take a ride in his car. Lakey accepted, not even knowing his name.

Evidently, both believed in love at first sight, because

they had instantly become its willing victims. In the car, they told each other that they had been hit by lightning and were hopelessly in love. Then they turned to each other and asked, "By the way, what's your name?"

Since their love had peaked so soon, it was only natural that things should go downhill from there. Bucky waited a full week before calling his newfound love. Both continued dating other people. Whatever the reason for this strange behavior, their apparent inability to communicate openly about the genuinely strong feelings they had for one another created a vicious cycle that was to impact a lifetime.

Bucky told Lakey's family that he planned on marrying their daughter, but he omitted a small detail—telling *her.* Lakey's family wasn't big in the communication department either, as they failed or forgot to convey this important detail to her as well. Bucky had given Lakey his "Silver Wings" pin, that he had earned and which to *him* clearly meant that they were engaged. Unfortunately, no one explained the significance of the "Wings" to Lakey, and she thought Bucky didn't care deeply enough to marry her.

Bucky went off to fight in World War II from 1941 to 1946. He wrote many letters to Lakey, but never once expressed his love for her, and never ventured to ask the all-important question, "Will you please wait for me?" Lakey responded to Bucky's letters, trying to read his emotions and intentions between the lines, but his correspondence frustrated her, yielding no clues. Finally, deciding that he wasn't serious about her, Lakey stopped postponing her life. Ultimately, Bucky received a "Dear John" letter from her, telling him that she was now married to George "Cush" Foster.

When Bucky came home from the war, there wasn't a large pool of women to date. Most of the local girls had already gotten married. Hanging around with some friends in the delis on North Park Heights Avenue, he bumped into a woman named Edna, whom he had met before the war. They started dating, and Bucky never had to ask "Will you marry me?"—Edna did it for him. Edna even went and got the marriage license on her own.

Even as the years passed, neither Bucky nor Lakey had ever gotten each other completely out of their systems. Bucky often spoke of Lakey to his wife, and told her that he wished he could talk to her just once. Edna gave him permission to go ahead, but of course, he never acted on it. Likewise, Lakey had also told her husband, Cush, about her first love, Bucky. Cush shrugged and said he didn't feel competitive, because, after all, *he* was the one married to her, wasn't he? But if she ever saw Bucky, he told her, it would be OK for her to talk to him. The possibility of Bucky and Lakey actually meeting was dim because the Fosters lived in Harrisburg, Pennsylvania, and the Beckers were in Bucky's home town of Baltimore. The distance grew even greater when in 1971 Lakey and Cush moved to Los Angeles to be near their daughter, Lois, and her family.

In October 1999, Lakey's sister, Libby, moved to a

new apartment in Baltimore. One month later, someone knocked at her door and asked if she was by any chance the former Libby Holcomb? The man making the inquiry was none other than Bucky. Of all the apartment complexes in Baltimore, Libby had moved into the same building where Bucky was currently living!

Bucky told Libby that his wife, Edna, has passed away the year before, after fifty-four years of marriage. He asked Libby to give him Lakey's phone number and address. He just wanted to talk to her for old times' sake, he said. Libby didn't think that Lakey had anything to fear from an eighty-year-old, so she told him how to reach her sister.

Lakey's husband, Cush, was now living in a nursing home, fading fast from Alzheimer's disease, which had begun eight years earlier. Long before Bucky tried contacting Lakey, she had already made plans to visit her siblings in January 2000. She was reluctant to leave her husband even for a few days, but all of her siblings were now in their eighties, and she felt she shouldn't postpone the trip. Her daughter, son, and grandchildren assured her that they would take care of Cush while she was gone and pushed her to go.

One month before Lakey was scheduled to leave on her trip, Cush passed away at the age of ninety-one. The idea of a trip to Baltimore seemed like a bad idea to Lakey, who was still in mourning, but everyone encouraged her to go. Besides, staying in L.A. only heightened her grief and sadness, and a visit to Baltimore would offer a welcome distraction.

In Baltimore, Lakey's siblings—joined by a newcomer who was almost like family—waited impatiently for her. In his arms, Bucky held a dozen red roses, and on the front door of her sister's apartment, he had painted a sign reading "Welcome Shanghai Lil!"—a song that had been popular during World War II and the nickname he had used for her some sixty years before.

Bucky and Lakey talked and talked. Lakey had only two weeks in Baltimore, but the two made the most of the little time they had. Trying not to offend or ignore Lakey's siblings (the reason for her trip!), they kept company constantly. Bucky belonged to a breakfast club called "Romeo" (Retired Old Men Eating Out) that met at a restaurant every day. They welcomed Lakey with open arms and made her the only female member.

Bucky took Lakey to meet his doctor, his banker, and a friend who writes for a newspaper. The friend wanted to know why Bucky was so happy. Bucky explained how he had found his true love again . . . after sixty years. The writer wanted to print their story, but Lakey asked him to wait since it was so soon after Cush had passed away. Maybe next visit, she said.

Bucky and Lakey told their children about their reunion, and both sets were delighted for their respective parents. They only wanted their happiness—and how many couples find their long-lost loves after sixty-odd years? No one felt angry or betrayed. Bucky and Lakey had been excellent spouses and wonderful parents, and they deserved this miracle in the twilight of their lives.

Bucky and Lakey got married on August 28, 2000. Their children—and I am one of them—hope they are given long, happy, healthy lives together so that they can indeed make up for all the time they lost. ✿

—LOIS FOSTER HIRT

I was devastated when, early on in my marriage, doctors informed my husband and me that, because of my severe case of endometriosis, we would never be able to have children. So we were over-joyed when, several years later, our adoption papers came through and our new daughter was placed in our arms.

The years slipped by quickly. Before I knew it, we were celebrating Lauren's fifth birthday. When I tucked her into bed that night, I suddenly remembered the intense look of concentration that had appeared on her face as she blew out the candles on her birthday cake. I asked her what she had wished for. "If I tell you, my wish won't come true!" she protested. I reassured her that telling me would do her wish no harm whatsoever. Finally, she confided in me. What she really wanted, she said, was a baby brother!

My husband Don and I both came from large families and we did not want Lauren to miss out on growing up with siblings. We had applied for our second adoption almost as soon as we were legally allowed. Four years passed, and my last call from the agency hadn't sounded promising.

A few days later, while Lauren and I were out shopping, she picked up a pair of pink, frilly baby booties.

"Can we get these for the baby?" she asked.

"Honey, we aren't going to have a baby. Besides, those shoes are for girls. I thought you wanted a brother."

"I can't decide. My friend Chris says it's pretty cool having a little brother. Well, most of the time anyway. But I've been thinking a little sister might be kind of fun. I have changed my mind—I want both!"

"Both," I repeated, rolling my eyes.

A few months later, we received a surprise call from the adoption agency. We now had a son. Lauren named him Tommy after her favorite character from the *Rugrats* cartoon.

That must have been some wish Lauren made, because the month before her sixth birthday, I confounded doctors by giving birth to a healthy baby girl.

I have no doubt that Lauren loves her brother and sister, but whenever she starts to complain about them getting into her things or pestering her, I just smile and remind her: "You asked for them!"

The youngest, Grace, turned three today. We finished singing "Happy Birthday" and told her to make a wish and then blow out her candles. Before Grace had a chance to do so, Lauren whispered in her ear: "Be careful what you wish for, kid." ❧

—CINDY ROBERT

*M*y husband and I were married on a shoestring budget. To compound matters, our expenses seemed to converge all at once: I was finishing a long period of dental work; we needed to buy a car; my husband's job transferred him to a new location; and we had to find an apartment and furniture. My savings account had been depleted in order to pay for the wedding. We knew this was going to be a rough year.

I worked two jobs, teaching during the week and clerking weekends at a department store. My husband had a regular job, plus working as a tutor on weekends. We hardly saw each other. "Ships passing in the night" was the catchphrase that described our marriage.

My father had died of leukemia two years before I met my husband. Medical bills had eaten away at my family's savings. My mother couldn't cope with the task of going through my father's financial records for a year after I was married. Finally, however, during one of her weekly phone calls to me, she mentioned that she was now emotionally ready to face them and would indeed start tackling them that evening.

That night, I had an unusual dream in which my father was trying to hand something to me that had small blue flowers wrapped around it. He kept trying to push aside a gauzy curtain to reach through, but he just couldn't seem to do it. Each time he tried, he receded and receded until he disappeared. I woke up at 4 A.M. in a cold sweat. The dream was so real, it took me a minute to realize where I was. I had goose bumps for days afterward.

My husband and I were now nearing our first wedding anniversary. My husband's employer wanted to send him to San Francisco to take part in a training program, and would cover his expenses. Wives were permitted to accompany their spouses, provided they paid their own way. The round-trip fare was $165.27—an enormous sum to us, as we were still paying back all the debt we had accumulated on dental bills and furniture. There was no way I could afford to go along, and sadly, my husband declined on my behalf.

Several days later, my mother phoned to say that she had found an insurance policy in the old files. Apparently, my father had taken it out on himself when they had first married. He had kept the policy up for five years and then had stopped paying on it. My mother phoned the company to ask what to do. They requested both a copy of the death certificate and the old policy.

Several weeks later, my mother phoned to say that a

check had arrived in the mail and she was sending it to me. I said "No," but she insisted. When the check arrived, I was astonished to see that it was for $165.27 — exactly to the penny the amount of money needed for the San Francisco trip. The check from the insurance company had blue flowers on it. And it wasn't too late to accept the travel offer from my husband's firm.

For several days, while my husband attended classes, I got to see San Francisco—from Nob Hill to Chinatown to Muir Woods to the Bay. What a wonderful first wedding anniversary gift from someone who couldn't be there! ❀

—MARIE ASNER

$\mathcal{M}$y great-great-grandfather, Rabbi Chaim Halberstam, was a renowned sage known as *The Sanzer Rebbe* (named after the Polish town of *Sanz*, where he lived), celebrated throughout Europe for his wisdom, charity, and piety. In the late nineteenth century, young men married early, and when Chaim was still a teenager, his parents sought an appropriate match for him. He had already acquired a local reputation as an *ilui* (a genius), and the most venerable family patriarchs were eager to have him as a son-in-law. However, some of their daughters were unwilling.

For, despite his sterling character, his sharp mind, his religious fervor, and his famous acts of kindness, Chaim had one flaw that made young women wary. He had been born with one leg slightly shorter than the other, and consequently walked with a pronounced limp. While prospective fathers-in-law dismissed the slight handicap as insignificant, their daughters faltered. Soon, his parents discovered that it was not as easy to marry him off as they had originally hoped, despite all his meritorious qualities.

One day, when his parents informed him that a notable rabbi's daughter had declined a match with him, he asked the rabbi for permission to personally argue his case with the young woman. He had something of great importance to tell her, he said.

"You know," he said gently to her when the meeting had been arranged, "that the Talmud says that forty days before children are born, Heaven decrees whom they will marry. 'So and so will be married to so and so,' a heavenly voice rings out. You know this, right?"

"Yes," she answered softly, with downcast, modest eyes.

"Well, before I was born, my soul asked to see my destined one. And when I saw you, my soul sang, because you were so perfect. Except for one thing."

"What was that?" she asked, curious.

"A limp. You had a terrible, pronounced limp, because one of your legs was shorter than the other. And I felt such pain that a beautiful, perfect thing like you should have this handicap. And I knew how much more appearances matter to women than to men, and how terrible it would be for you to carry this handicap all your life. So my soul begged heaven: 'Please, please give the handicap to me, instead. Let me be afflicted with this disability instead of my beloved.'

"Heaven was moved by my sacrifice for you and gave *me* the limp instead. This is why I have the limp today, and you do not. I took it upon myself so that you would not suffer."

The young woman was quiet and left the room without saying a word.

Later that night, she approached her father and said that she had changed her mind. It would be an honor, she said, to marry Chaim Halberstam.

The two did indeed marry, and they had many children who followed faithfully in their father's footsteps. Sons assumed their father's mantle of greatness, and their sons after that. An international rabbinic dynasty was established that exists to this day, and I feel privileged to be among its progeny. ❀

—YITTA HALBERSTAM

The sun shone brightly on the ocean from the azure skies of Key West, Florida, but clouds and rain would have better suited the situation that my mother and father found themselves in some seventy years ago.

Hector, my older brother, was fifteen at the time, and had contracted a potentially blinding eye disease that was not only contagious but required surgery if it was to be cured. Because of the danger of infecting his classmates, the school authorities had barred Hector from attending school until he had undergone the surgery required to heal the condition. Our family was poor, and we worried about obtaining even the bare necessities. A procedure of this magnitude was something my parents, Josefa and Oscar, simply couldn't afford. Yet they feared that my brother Delio (who was twelve) and I (seven at the time) would contract the eye disease from Hector.

My mother was a woman of great faith, and she prayed constantly that God would help her and my father find the money for the necessary surgery. As the days passed, they became desperate to find a solution to the problem.

One night my mother had a vivid dream in which she distinctly saw the number 36. When she awoke, she knew that she must place a bet on this number in the local *bolita* (lottery). Now, my mother had never gambled before in her life and did not approve of the activity, but my brother's serious eye condition required drastic measures. So the morning after her strange dream, she instructed my father to place a bet on the number 36.

The next day, my mother was standing on our balcony, anxiously waiting for my father to come home, to bring news of whether or not she had the winning number.

After waiting in the glaring Florida sun for what seemed like an eternity, my mother finally spied my father walking up the street. Her heart raced with anticipation. My father suddenly stopped beneath the balcony, gazed up at her with a strange look on his face and shouted, "Honey, you hit the number 36!" My mother fell to her knees and prayed in gratitude.

As it turned out, not only was the number that had appeared in her dream a winning number, but the win had brought them the exact amount of money needed for Hector's operation.

Even after seventy years, this story continues to be told as our family's own special miracle—perhaps a "tip" from God, delivered via my mother's prophetic dream. ✿

—TERESA CRUZ GUZMAN

*T*hey both roamed the school corridors at the same time: he was a security guard, and she was a student. While he was patrolling the hallways for safety, she was using them as her base of operations to stop and talk to friends, laugh and flirt with guys, and exchange smiles and waves with teachers. The guard and the student were probably within feet—or perhaps inches—of each other many times throughout the school day. But both were completely innocent of any unusual connection between them. How could they envision that a life-changing drama was about to unfold simply because of the astuteness of one faculty member in their midst?

"Hey," Tautkus, the band teacher at the San Diego high school, said to the man he knew only as "Chuck the security guard." "You asked me the other day about joining the Masons. Well, it just so happens that one of my students, a girl named Heather, told me in conversation that her father had just become a member of the lodge. So I asked her how one goes about applying for membership, and she gave me all the info you need. Lucky coincidence, huh?"

"Gee, thanks man, I really appreciate it," Chuck said. "That is kinda weird, me asking you about the Masons and then your student telling you her father just joined."

"Come to think of it, what's even *weirder*," said Tautkus, peering at Chuck and considering him thoughtfully, "is that the two of you look so much alike, she could pass as your daughter!"

"Hey, I'm too old to have a teenage daughter," Chuck joked back. "How about a *granddaughter*? What's her name?"

"Heather Perry," Tautkus replied.

Chuck was silent for a moment as his face turned white.

"Hey, Tautkus," he said, casually. "You don't actually know my last name, do you? Well, my last name also happens to be Perry. You don't by any chance know her father's *first name*, do you?"

"I happen to know the family well, Chuck. Heather's dad's first name is Charles."

"Well, Tautkus, surprise! So is mine. Chuck is my nickname. Tautkus, I think you've just found me my long-lost son, whom I haven't seen in thirty-five years!"

That evening, Charles Perry Senior, who all these years had been fearful of tracking down his son and daughters for fear of rejection—he had disappeared from his family's life after he had divorced their mother—

dialed a phone number with trembling hands.

"Charles Perry?" he said into the answering machine. "My name is also Charles Perry. If you'll give me a call, I think you might find that we have something in common. . . ." ❀

*S*ixty years ago, on the banks of a muddy river in the Philippine jungle, a young man begged a fellow soldier to grant him a dying wish.

"I want you to do something for me," Howard Leachman told a startled Glenn Frazier. "I'm dying."

Both men were prisoners of war, captured during the Japanese conquest of the Philippines.

They had survived the infamous Bataan Death March, only to be put to work as slave laborers on a road detail.

Leachman, gasping to speak, fished out from his mud-caked wallet a worn photograph of a baby boy.

"This is my son, who was born after I left Fort Benning," he said. "I want you to promise to go back and make sure he's being taken care of. Tell him about me and how much I loved him."

Frazier, then just seventeen, made the promise.

Almost six decades later, he was finally able to keep it.

In an emotional reunion in Atlanta, Frazier met Leachman's son, Howard Marshall, a sixty-two-year-old Atlanta scientist. Their meeting has helped both men come to grips with a painful past, and provided Marshall with the unexpected chance to find many of his father's relatives, people he hadn't known existed. The men's meeting was "very painful, but also wonderful," Marshall says. "To know that when he died, my daddy was thinking of me, after all he went through . . ."

"I never thought it would happen," adds Frazier seventy-seven, a decorated army veteran who drove from Florida to Marshall's home in Atlanta for their first meeting. "It was one of the most gratifying things I have ever done."

Frazier made the promise to Marshall's father during one of the darkest periods of World War II. Frazier and Leachman had been captured along with more than 10,000 other GIs on the Philippines' Bataan Peninsula, just months after the Japanese attack on Pearl Harbor. Their forced march to a prisoner of war camp became known as the Bataan Death March.

Both were plucked out of the surviving POW pool for a 306-man work detail carving a road out of the jungle. In less than three months of work, more than half of the men, including Leachman, died of malaria, dysentery, dengue fever, starvation, or exhaustion. Frazier, however, was eventually transferred to a POW camp in Japan.

Returning to the United States after the war ended in 1945, he contacted the Leachman family in Cartersville, Georgia. Frazier was assured that the child was being cared for, but the family didn't want to discuss the still raw subject of Leachman's death. Which meant Frazier wasn't able to tell the son about the dying man's requests, an important part of his promise.

Frazier figured he'd done all he could.

By that time, Howard Marshall was living with his mother, who had married another man in a distant part of Georgia. Time and circumstance soon obscured his Cartersville connections. Marshall eventually earned a doctorate in marine sciences, married, and had children of his own.

He's not sure why, but earlier this year, Marshall felt a "real pulling urge" to learn more about his biological father.

"I had sort of avoided it for a long time," he says. "But a few months ago, I started reading all I could about Bataan, hoping I could find out something about my daddy. I couldn't find anything."

Then serendipity intervened.

Marshall and his wife, Gail, were visiting a friend who's a genealogist and they mentioned his quest to find some information about his father.

"She went on her computer and a day or two later called me back with information," Marshall says. "She told me he was listed as MIA (missing in action), which was disturbing because that was contrary to what Mama had said."

Marshall, doing some research of his own, found out about Michael Norman, a New York University professor who was researching the work detail that claimed Leachman's life. Norman e-mailed Marshall the names of nine known survivors of the work detail.

One was Paul Reuter, a leader of the American Defenders of Bataan. Marshall contacted him. "He took my information and said, 'If I ever talk to someone who was there, I'll ask them about your daddy.'"

By chance, just a day later, Frazier called Reuter for some information regarding an article in a veterans' newsletter.

Reuter asked Frazier for any names he remembered from the work detail.

"Leachman," Frazier replied.

"Well, you're not going to believe this, but I just talked to Leachman's son yesterday," Reuter told him. "He's in the Atlanta area."

Frazier, who says he had "never stopped thinking" about his unfulfilled promise, called Marshall right away.

"He almost fainted, and so did I," Frazier says. "I could tell he needed to ask those little-boy questions about his daddy that had always been inside him. And I knew I could tell him things he didn't know."

What Frazier told him was horrific, Marshall says. "There was malaria and dying and dengue fever. No good food, and not enough of that."

Then Frazier told Marshall about his father's last moment, a hard story for the veteran to tell and for the son to hear.

Stricken and separated from Frazier, Leachman had desperately asked friends to find his buddy. Frazier had sneaked past Japanese guards to find the dying man.

"He was gasping. He was sort of delirious but said: 'I want you to do something for me.' He showed me this picture and begged me to check after the baby . . . I had to leave, but in a day or two I got word again. My guts told me, 'You better prepare yourself now; he's about gone.'"

They were right.

"He sort of whispered, 'Please do as you promised,'" Frazier remembers. "I said, 'I will.' He said, 'Now I'll die in peace.' It was just a minute or so, and I couldn't find his pulse."

Now both men want to have Leachman's body located, exhumed, identified, and returned to Cartersville. "It would be a miracle to find him, but anything's possible," according to NYU professor Norman.

Marshall—and his newfound uncles, aunts and cousins—are optimistic.

"We want him home," the son says. "We all want him home. And in the family plot, together with his mother and father. We're going to make every effort to get him there."

Frazier is eager to help, and almost gleeful that he was at last able to fulfill his promise completely.

"I feel I got more out of this than Howard," he says. "I got a lasting friend, and I've finally done my duty." ❀

Reprinted with permission from the *Atlanta Journal Constitution*, November 3, 2000, by Bill Hendrick, page E1, "A Dying Wish Fulfilled Nearly Six Decades Later."

$\mathcal{I}$f ever there seemed a woman destined for motherhood, it was Annie. From the time that she had been a toddler, she had always reached lovingly for those younger and smaller than herself. She would squeal in delight whenever one of her mother's friends came visiting with babies, her warm brown eyes crinkling up in happy smiles as she gently planted ardent kisses on the infants' foreheads. And she always offered to "baby-sit," even though she was barely out of diapers herself. Despite Annie's own tender age, somehow her mother's friends trusted her from the start. Squalling infants calmed down the moment they were placed in her arms and began cooing contentedly. "That little girl sure has a knack," the adults would comment as they watched her, awestruck. "She has MOM stamped all over her."

Even her name seemed to be a harbinger of the future that awaited her. The name "Annie" was somehow redolent of the fragrant smell of freshly baked cookies, old-fashioned aprons dusted with flour, steaming cups of hot cocoa on lazy Saturday mornings. "Wait till she gets married," the adults who watched her promised one another with absolute certitude. "She'll have a brood of kids."

Alas, it was not meant to be. Annie got married young enough—just nineteen—and, true to the predictions made about her long ago, wanted nothing more than the white picket fence and a minivan crammed with children. Her young husband, Cliff, had a responsible job and was happy to start a family right away. Annie's parents, in-laws, friends, and neighbors waited for the young couple to announce the good news almost as soon as they were married. Fate, however, had decreed otherwise.

"I had a miscarriage," Annie whispered over the phone to her best friend, Leslie, who lived 3,000 miles away.

"You'll get pregnant again real soon, I'm sure," Leslie promised. She had been on the verge of confiding a secret to Annie—the reason for her call—but Annie had blurted out her own news first. Sensitive to her friend's misery, she knew this clearly wasn't the right time. She would have to tell her eventually, but she certainly couldn't *now*. How could any decent human being—at the height of her best friend's despair about the loss of a first baby—tell her that she was expecting her own?

Annie and Leslie had been best friends for over ten years, and had shared almost everything in their lives. They had been all of nine when they first met, and had grown up together, experiencing life's milestones at practically the same time. They had gotten their first periods, first training bras, and first kisses almost simultaneously, and it was exciting for them to undergo these female adventures together. As naïve youngsters who thought they could write life's scripts, they plotted their futures together. *We'll get married to brothers, live in the same house, and be pregnant and have our babies at the same time!* they hoped. Of course, real life rarely accords with fantasy, and ultimately, they had married men who were strangers to one another and they had moved to opposite coasts. And it also appeared that Leslie was going to have the first baby . . . alone.

"It's actually a good sign that you had a miscarriage," Leslie said over the phone with a catch in her voice. "Doctors always say that. It means you're fertile; it means you can have children."

But over the years, Leslie was proven wrong. Leslie kept on getting pregnant, Annie kept on having miscarriages. Annie and Cliff spared no expenses in trying to conceive: They traveled all over the world to consult with fertility specialists who might offer them a new treatment or a glimmer of hope. But none did. Leslie began feeling guilty each time she became pregnant again, and hid her news from Annie for as long as she could. Instead of the symmetries and synchronicities they had experienced when they were young, the best friends' trajectories couldn't have been more different.

"Another miscarriage," Annie would whisper over and over again to Leslie as the years flew by.

"Another pregnancy," Leslie would restrain herself from announcing, waiting to tell her friend until the propitious time.

There never was any really propitious time. If there was anything they did in sync, it was Leslie's pregnancies and Annie's miscarriages. Leslie knew that Annie felt happy for her, but still, Annie was human, wasn't she? She had to feel the slightest twinge, if not much more, didn't she? Leslie ached for her friend. She wished that she had the power to give her what she wanted more than anything else in the world: children.

People finally began to suggest to Annie that she adopt, but she said she just couldn't. She wanted her own, she told them. She was going to keep on trying and never give up. Meanwhile, she took a job at the local nursery school, where she parlayed her love for children into a successful teaching career.

Leslie had seven pregnancies that bore fruit. Annie had seven that didn't. How far their plans—and fates— had diverged!

But everything—even Annie's heartbreaking infertility—dimmed to insignificance when Leslie called the next time with *her* news.

"Breast cancer," she said with a tremor. "The doctor says it's pretty advanced."

"I'll be there tomorrow," Annie said.

Annie took a leave of absence from her job and flew to California to be with her friend. Leslie's husband,

Joey, had his hands full caring for seven kids—ranging in age from six months to fourteen years—and accompanying Leslie to her radiation treatments. Annie took over running the household, and, in a perverse twist of fate, finally saw the dreams of her childhood realized. She was ferrying carloads of jostling kids back and forth to school and to lessons and appointments; baking mouth-watering delicacies for hungry young mouths to feed on; singing nursery songs and reciting poems and telling stories at bedtime. Underneath her cheery demeanor was a terrible ache. *Please get better, Leslie,* she begged inside. *We all need you and love you so much.*

But the radiation didn't help, and the next, last, desperate step in treatment was a bone marrow transplant. Leslie flew to Denver together with Joey, and left her kids in the care of her best friend since youth.

"See ya soon," Leslie promised Annie and the kids before she left for the airport.

But she never did.

Leslie died in Denver, and when she did, a certain part of Joey—her devoted husband of fifteen years—died with her. Almost immediately after Leslie's death, Joey became disoriented and irrational; his eyes glazed over and his sentences were muddled and disjointed. The doctors put him on medication and under observation, but his progress was dismal. "He'll have to be institutionalized," they told Annie. He wasn't coming back to California for a long time, they said.

Leslie's parents and in-laws were both dead. Leslie and her husband had no siblings. "What's going to happen to the kids?" she asked.

In New York, Annie's husband Cliff had begun losing patience. His wife had been gone for over five months, and as much as he had compassion for Leslie and her family, he wanted his wife back. "You have been an amazing, wonderful, devoted friend to Leslie," he told his wife, "and what you've done for her and her family has been incredible, but it's time to come home."

"Honey, *you've* been incredible," she told her husband, "and I know I'm asking a lot, but I can't just abandon them like this."

"Well, talk to their lawyer or whoever is in charge, and make arrangements. I want you home, Annie!"

On the phone, Annie frantically conferred with the doctors in Denver. "What is Joey's condition?" she asked. "Is he getting any better?"

"Actually," the doctors replied with regret, "there seems to be a downward spiral here. He's getting worse."

One day, two professionally dressed women in suits rang Leslie's doorbell and asked to see Annie and the children. They were from an agency, they said, that had been mandated by the state to place Leslie's kids in foster homes until such time as their father was psychologically capable of taking care of them himself.

"You mean foster *home*, don't you?" Annie asked with a quaver in her voice. "You said foster *homes*. You *are* going to put them into *one* home, aren't you?"

The women blinked at her naïve assumption.

"Oh, no," one of them said. "That's impossible. Where would we find one family to take seven children? We're going to place each one in a different home."

"But they're *siblings*," Annie protested. "They're each other's family. They're all they've got now. You can't separate them!"

"Really!" one of the women exclaimed in disbelief. "Now where exactly would we find one home that wants to take in *seven children*?"

Annie called her husband that night. "Cliff? There's something we have to discuss."

Annie and Cliff opened their hearts and home to Leslie's kids and officially became their foster parents. Later, when it sadly became clear that Joey would never fully recover from his illness, they formally adopted all seven. They raised all of them lovingly, and strangers unfamiliar with the story never had cause to suspect that they were not their biological children.

Today, Leslie's kids are all married and have children of their own. And these children call Cliff and Annie "Gramps" and "Grandma," as they are the only ones they have ever known. And Annie wears old-fashioned aprons coated with flour, bakes homemade cookies, and prepares steaming cups of hot cocoa for the grandkids who jostle each other in her worn minivan, as she ferries them from school to lessons to appointments. All of her children live nearby, and Annie gets to see her grandchildren almost every day.

In so many of their young faces, she sees traces of Leslie, and they are poignant reminders of her special friend.

"I wish I had the power to give you children," Leslie had once said.

If only it hadn't been this way, Annie often thought. *But in a way . . . you did.*

$\mathcal{M}$yriam Fuchs of Brooklyn, New York, traveled to Jerusalem in December 2001 to visit her married daughter Ruchama, who was expecting her first child and experiencing some discomfort during her pregnancy. The presence of her mother would soothe her greatly, Ruchama confessed over the telephone in a small, scared voice, and Myriam made flight arrangements posthaste. She knew that the State Department had issued a travel advisory warning American tourists to stay away from Israel while the "Rosh Hashanah Intifada" raged on, but she dismissed the slight fears that prickled at her. Besides, if Israel was safe enough for her married daughter to live in—and her youngest daughter Rochel to study in—it was certainly safe enough for her to visit. So Myriam packed her bags, squelched her apprehension, and took off for the Holy Land to bring succor and mother love to two children far away from home.

After about a week of ministering to her pregnant daughter's needs, Myriam decided she was due for a night out on the town. In Jerusalem—spiritual center of the world—nightlife, or at least nightlife the way Westerners know it, is severely restricted. Popular Saturday night activities for married Orthodox couples typically include either attending enriching educational lectures or dining out at a café or restaurant. Myriam and her younger daughter Rochel (who was studying at a women's institute in Israel) opted for Café Rimon, a kosher restaurant located in the heart of *Ben Yehuda*, a bustling outdoor pedestrian mall.

Four months after the tragic Sbarro Pizza bombing in Jerusalem, pedestrians had finally returned to the streets, and business on *Ben Yehuda* was brisk. The pedestrian mall was filled with foreign students, Israeli citizens, and a few stray tourists. Café Rimon overflowed with patrons and hummed with laughter, excited chatter, and music. *Israelis are such a resilient people,* Myriam thought, as she and her daughter hunted for a vacant table. Myriam welcomed the noise, the throngs, and the congestion. It actually felt good to wade through the crush and have to worry about securing a table. This was much better than the empty streets that had stretched before the store-keepers' stricken eyes for so many endless weeks.

"I'm starving!" Myriam announced to Rochel as they grabbed the last remaining table. "Sorry," she apologized to the disappointed couple who had also made a beeline for the same table, just a beat too late. She turned to Rochel, "I haven't eaten since Sabbath lunch—what about you? Have you ever tried their French onion soup? Deelish!" She waved to a nearby waiter and beckoned him close. The waiter took their order promptly, but warned that there was a backlog in the kitchen. "We had to let a lot of our staff go in recent months," he explained, "and we weren't prepared for the crowd tonight. I'll try to bring your order as soon as possible," he promised.

"Please!" Myriam urged, "I'm starving!"

The waiter had warned them, but they were not quite prepared for *such* an interminable wait. "How long does it take to ladle soup into a bowl?" Myriam grumbled. "It's been more than a half hour since the waiter took our order!"

Just as the waiter finally emerged from the kitchen, heading in their direction and bearing aloft the ceramic crocks of fragrant soup for which Café Rimon was so renowned, Myriam's cell phone rang. It was her pregnant daughter, Ruchama.

"Ma!" she wailed. "I don't feel so well. Please come home."

Myriam longingly eyed the bed of cheese and miniature croutons floating in the sea of steaming soup, and told Ruchama: "Sweetheart, we're sitting at Café Rimon and just got our order. I'll come as soon as we finish, OK?"

"Ma, you don't understand. I really don't feel well."

"We'll eat real fast and we won't order anything else, OK?" Myriam begged. "Be there soon."

But Ruchama wasn't placated. Instead, her voice became shrill with alarm and impatience. "Ma, I can't wait. I need you. *Now!*"

Myriam stole one last yearning glance at the soup, threw some bills down on the table, motioned to the waiting couple still hovering nearby that they were leaving, and rushed with Rochel down the mall toward the nearest taxi stop. The two had not yet left the area when they heard a terrifying explosion accompanied by a cacophony of sounds: screams, cries, and sirens. The faces of pedestrians that just moments before had been so carefree and cheerful now blanched in shock and horror as they sobbed into one another's arms: "It's a *pegua* — a terrorist attack. Near a restaurant. Café Rimon." As the words registered with Myriam and her daughter, they regarded each other with stunned disbelief and fled into the night.

The next morning, Myriam made a pilgrimage back to Café Rimon, where the cleanup had already begun. The damage was extensive and sobering. The bomb had exploded directly in front of the restaurant and several patrons had been killed and injured. Myriam anticipated finding a boarded-up storefront; the rubble that only last night had been tables and chairs; the bleak, despairing faces of the staff as they milled around helplessly. But with typical Israeli resilience that was so inbred in the national character, the chaos of the night before had been swept away, and the restaurant was open for business.

Myriam sought out the waiter who had served her table the night before and was relieved to learn that he was unhurt. After ascertaining that he had escaped injury, she pressed on with the second question that had tormented her all night. What, she wanted to know, had happened to the young couple that had seized her table just as she left?

"I don't know how to tell you this, Madam," the waiter said, averting his eyes. "This was a catastrophe. The young man who took your seat . . . he died instantly. I don't know who or what made you get up from your table so suddenly, but whatever it was, it was a blessing for you. Your life was spared as a result."

When Myriam told Ruchama that her phone call had saved her life, Myriam's daughter said: "See, Ma? I'm your angel."

"That you are," Myriam replied with a shiver. "That you surely are." ❀

*T*he names of both the mother and the child have been lost to history, but the name of the good Samaritan — albeit an unwitting one — has been preserved. He was known as Joseph Figlock, and he had the unusual distinction of being someone's savior — although he didn't really have much say in the matter, as we will find out as the story unfolds.

In the 1930s, "childproofing" one's home was not as commonplace as it is today, and such paraphernalia as gates and guardrails were not widely used. Children's safety depended more on the careful scrutiny and quick reflexes of parents than anything else. In the 1920s, the parent at home was almost always the mother. Sometimes, though, the mothers were so young, so inexperienced, or just so plain overwhelmed that it was inevitable for their watchful eyes to droop in weariness. It only takes one split-second distraction — a ringing telephone, a buzzing doorbell, the cry of another child — and the scene is set for the worst to happen. Ultimately, in this case, the cause is unknown and unimportant. What is critical is what transpired next.

Joseph Figlock was walking down a street in Detroit when a baby suddenly plunged headlong from the window of an upper-floor apartment. Fortuitously, the baby landed on Joseph, bringing *him* down, and together they both tumbled to the ground, Joseph underneath the baby, cushioning its fall. The screaming mother ran out from the building, seized the uninjured baby, thanked Joseph—shaken but unharmed—and blessed God, all in one breath. Joseph was thrilled to have been able to save the baby's life—for that is surely what he unwittingly did—but he was stunned by the sudden sequence of events.

From his perspective, it felt as if the sky had suddenly rained babies down upon him. After a crowd gathered and reporters descended on the scene, he was elevated to the status of a hero. Joseph protested that he had done nothing heroic; it was all in the timing, he insisted. But the baby's mother proclaimed that he alone had saved her baby's life.

The saying goes that lightning never strikes twice in the same place, but real life doesn't heed aphorisms. Exactly one year later, the very same baby (now a toddler) fell from the very same window onto the very same man, who was once again passing underneath at the perfect moment. Yes, it was none other than poor, unsuspecting Joseph Figlock, who seemed to have developed a penchant for being in the right place at the right time.

The scenario was almost precisely the same as the previous year. Joseph's body broke the baby's fall, the baby (older and plumper) temporarily flattened him, and both emerged unscathed from the incident.

No one knows whether Joseph Figlock ever walked down that street again. Perhaps he thought it would be prudent to try a different route. All we can assume is that the baby's mother was eternally grateful. ✯

"I'm a throwback to a different era," he would often laugh self-deprecatingly. "A relic."

"I *love* your top hat," she would respond loyally. "It's adorable!"

"Still," he'd say hesitantly, "people look at me strangely when I wear it."

"Oh, what do you care what people say or think?" she'd say, pooh-poohing his insecurity. "What matters most is what *you* think."

"Well, I do maintain that people should get dressed up for church services! Formal, you know. The casual dress people favor these days seems to be an outright sacrilege!"

"You wear what you want, honey," she would soothe.

"I *do* love my top hat!" he'd say as he checked himself in the mirror before gallantly offering her his hand. "It's become my trademark, my signature, my calling card. I just can't part with it."

And out the door they'd go, arm in arm, every Sunday morning, he with his quirky top hat perched jauntily on his head.

For forty years, the Winstons had had the exact same conversation every Sunday morning as they prepared to go to church. The top hat had belonged to Bill's father, and was a throwback to an era that seemed to have disappeared. "People used to dress up to go to the opera and ballet and Broadway shows," he'd grumble, "in ballgowns and tuxedoes! But *today*," he'd shake his head in despair, "I can't believe what people consider proper attire for church services!"

As his faithful wife, Christina knew that these remarks really reflected her husband's anxiety about his top hat. He was not as concerned about the inappropriateness of *other* people's attire as he was of his own.

"Just wear your top hat, honey," she would laugh.

And for four decades, he did. Every Sunday morning to church.

But the day came, much too soon, when Christina walked to church alone. She had always hoped that her death would precede Bill's—she didn't think she could bear life without him—but he had beaten her to it. He had died in her arms a few weeks before, his last words a reprise of all his faithful years: ". . . Love you forever . . . And I'll always be with you . . . Don't worry, you won't be alone . . ."

But alone is what Christina felt as she walked, noticing the couples marching purposefully together, the families sprawling over the sidewalks, as they all quickened their pace to get to church on time. *Everyone seems to have someone but me,* she thought with uncharacteristic self-pity. *Hey, you had him for forty years!* she scolded herself sharply, ashamed. *That's more than so many other people get!*

Christina was being swept along in the great wave of humanity making its way to church when she stepped off the curb. Suddenly, she heard a screech of brakes as a car careened down the street, headed directly toward her. No adrenaline pumped, no reflexes jumped. Instead of racing forward or retreating backward, she stood frozen in her tracks, like a deer caught in the headlights. She was paralyzed with fear and couldn't move. Someone in the crowd screamed, and then a strong arm grabbed her, pulling her to safety as the car whizzed by. Shaken out of her paralysis, Christina turned to thank her benefactor, but whoever it was had already gone. *A good Samaritan,* she thought gratefully. She started to cry, shocked to realize how a few seconds had separated her from serious injury or death.

People rushed over to her, concern written on their faces. "Are you all right?"

"Yes," she sobbed, embarrassed by her tears. "But where is the man who saved me? I want to thank him!"

People had seen her step off the curb and noticed the car careening down the street. But no one had seen the man pulling her to safety.

"I kind of thought you just ran back to the sidewalk yourself," offered a young woman.

"No," insisted Christina. "A man grabbed me from behind."

"I guess it happened too fast . . ." the young woman answered lamely. "Well, anyway, thank God you're OK."

"Thank God," Christina replied.

In church that morning, Christina's prayers were, of course, filled with extra ardor and meaning. Still, as the minister's sermon droned on endlessly, she couldn't help but wonder about the man who had saved her. *Wasn't it odd that after saving her, he hadn't checked to make sure she was OK? Well, maybe he was one of those hero types who prefer to remain anonymous,* she told herself. *But how come no one in the crowd noticed him?* she wondered. *Shouldn't at least one person have seen him? The whole thing is strange.*

But the mystery only deepened after services. Everyone filed out of his respective pew, but Christina remained rooted in hers, still puzzling over the near–car accident. It was then that she noticed the empty pew in front of her. Someone seemed to have left an article of clothing behind. *I'll just bring it over to the church's Lost and Found,* Christina thought, as she bent over the pew to retrieve it. Christina trembled when she saw what the object was. It was not a scarf or a sweater, as she had originally guessed when she first saw the blur of black with her faulty vision. It was none other than a *top hat* — an exact replica of the one Bill had worn.

Christina thought of the strong, muscular, undeniably male arm that had pulled her out of harm's way and again looked at the top hat that inexplicably sat in front of her. *I'll always be with you,* Bill had promised as he gazed one last time at his wife of forty years. *You'll never be alone*. And, as inexplicable as it all seemed, Christina knew instinctively that he had kept his pledge. He had, after all, left his calling card behind. ✿

On a cold day in Jerusalem in February 1995, I was coming home discouraged and worried from a meeting with my midwife. I was in the last weeks of pregnancy with my first child, and I had just received the unwelcome news that the baby was still in breech position (buttocks down), as she had been for a month already. I was afraid of the hazards of a breech birth. But more than that, I had dreamed of a natural birth without medical intervention. I had signed up to give birth at a hospital known for supporting women being in charge of their labor and delivery, and that was where I wanted to have my first child. However, I had been told that the hospital routinely did Caesarean sections for breech births, so I saw my vision of a natural birth fading away.

We had tried *everything* to get the baby to turn around: exercises, lying on my back with my legs elevated (not easy in the eighth month of pregnancy!), visualizations—even drawing a lit flashlight up my belly to encourage the baby to follow the light with her head.

With every day, I became more determined to somehow turn the baby around so that I would not have to go through a breech birth or Caesarean. Reluctantly, I decided to undergo the rather uncomfortable process called external version, in which a doctor turns the baby around from the outside, using his hands. This meant checking into another hospital and possibly giving birth early, since the hospital usually tried to induce labor after the version to prevent the baby from turning back around again. I would have to give up my midwife—since this second hospital did not allow private mid-wives—and the supportive atmosphere I had wanted, but at least I had a chance for a natural birth rather than a Caesarean section.

I made an appointment with a doctor at the hospital who specializes in external version. After a brief examination, he told me that yes, the baby was still head-up. Moreover, he said that the baby's buttocks were so firmly wedged into the pelvis that she was no longer likely to turn around by herself. So we decided to go ahead and schedule the version for a week later.

That evening, I talked with a friend who told me of one more thing I might try. She told me that a rabbi in Mea Shearim, the ultra-Orthodox section of Jerusalem, specialized in pregnancy and birth problems, and that he might be able to help me. The next day I traveled to Mea Shearim and found the shabby little building where the rabbi received people. In the crowded, musty waiting room, I waited for two hours before my turn finally came to go into the rabbi's chambers. When I pushed open the door, a very elderly man with a long, stringy beard and a cigarette in his hand motioned me to sit down. As soon as I told him that the baby was in breech position, he immediately scribbled something on a scrap of paper and handed it to me. It was the name of a spring outside Jerusalem called *Ein Sataf*. He said that I was to drink water from this spring three times, and that my husband was to bring me the water each time. With that, he dismissed me and called the next woman in line.

The next morning, a Friday morning, my husband and I borrowed a friend's car and drove to the spring. We followed the rabbi's instructions, all the while feeling rather silly. That night, I felt that the baby was quite active, but my mind was still focused on the upcoming operation the following week.

On Sunday morning, I went back to the hospital to have an ultrasound test done, in preparation for the version operation. All of a sudden, as the ultrasound technician moved the sensor over my pelvis, she exclaimed, "The baby's head is down!" Two weeks later, my daughter Sara Regina was born in a completely natural birth. ✿

— ESTHER FRUMKIN

*W*hat kind of community
service could the members
of my small church per-
form? We pondered the question long and hard. We
wanted to adopt a project that all of us could participate
in, but it had to be something each one of us could rea-
sonably manage—in terms of both effort and time. To
undertake something time-consuming and onerous
would be self-defeating; we would end up not doing it.

So, after much dialogue and deliberation, we finally
settled on what we called the Police Car Prayer Project.
We would pray for the police officers in our city—their
cars, and whatever kind of service they might be rendering in the community. We would also provide stuffed
toys to place in patrol cars for the officers to give to children who might be involved in an accident.

I signed up for the project and was directed to a list
of patrol car numbers posted on the bulletin board at the
church. Each one of us was asked to select a different
patrol car number for which we would individually pray.
I randomly chose police car number 211.

I had no idea who the officer was who drove that particular police car or where the car was assigned in our city. When I joined the prayer project, I was also asked to specify at what time of day I would regularly pray for the safety of the officer. I signed up for evening prayer because I felt that this was the most hazardous time of day, when a combination of the darkness, weather conditions, and increased traffic would impact the safety of the people in the community, as well as the police officer and his car.

However, I didn't stick to evening prayers only. Sometimes during the day—for no apparent reason—I'd suddenly have number 211 on my mind. I would stop whatever I was doing and momentarily pray for the safety of that car. One Sunday, I was on my way to lunch with friends, and we were going to the other side of town. As we were driving to the restaurant, I spotted, right in front of us, car number 211.

"There's my police car!" I told my friends. They were unfamiliar with the Police Car Prayer Project, so I took the opportunity to explain it to them. This was the first time I knew for certain that "my" patrol car was assigned to the other side of town. My prayers intensified from that point on. It felt as though I had "connected" with the driver of the car and, suddenly, prayer for the driver became more personal.

One day, I was at a meeting of my women's church group when I received a call on my cell phone from my daughter, Grace. There had been an accident, she said, near Grandma's house. Could I come quick? By the time I arrived at the scene, there were several police cars, an ambulance, a wrecker, and many people standing around. The car had been totaled. Grace was wet and cold, but otherwise OK. I thanked God that she was not hurt. "What happened?" I asked.

Grace had just gotten her driver's license, and had driven over to her grandmother's to show it off. My mother lived on a narrow road next to a creek. As Grace was leaving, the right front car wheel left the pavement and was caught by a water meter that was sticking up in the road. This caused the car to flip upside down in the creek. There was not very much water in the creek, which was a blessing. Grace crawled over the back seat of the car and was pulled to safety by the first responder to the accident. It was a miracle that she had escaped injury, everyone said.

I approached the police officer in charge to offer my gratitude for helping my daughter. She declined my effusive thanks, saying that it was someone else, not she, who had initially responded, but because it was shift change, he had already left the scene.

She comforted Grace and me, and we both felt blessed that Grace hadn't been injured, despite the fact that the car was completely wrecked.

The following day, I called the police station to find out how to receive a copy of the police report, which was needed in order to file the insurance claim. While I was on the telephone, I asked if there was any way they could track down the first responder to the accident.

"Sure. Hold on just a minute," the officer told me politely. She returned to the telephone. "It was number 211."

"I guess I already knew that before you told me," I said.

"Now how would you know that?" she asked. I told her about the Police Car Prayer Project and the coincidence of this incident.

I still pray for car number 211 every day, but I have expanded my prayers to include *all* police officers and firefighters, for we never know when or where an *incident* will become a *coincidence*. ❀

—Dr. Lynn R. Hartz

*I*n the early 1970s, I moved my young family into an old Victorian house in the city. The rooms were so large I could have put all of my furniture in two of them.

My father suggested that I start going to auctions and estate sales. Before long, I had a house full of wonderful old furniture, but I had been bitten by the antiquing bug. Now I couldn't stop! I became an addict. Every week my dad would call me with a list of upcoming auctions in the farming community where I grew up, and off I'd go.

Over the years, I collected many things, but my collection of old photographs was very dear to me. Most of the photographs were of beautiful Victorian women dressed in high-necked, crisp white blouses and long skirts with bustles. I often looked at the photographs and wondered about the special occasions for which they had been taken.

My favorite photograph was that of a girl. She was incredibly beautiful, with piercing dark eyes, thick dark curly hair, and creamy white skin.

In 1980, my family bought an old farmhouse in the

community where I grew up. I moved from the Victorian house in the city that had been so instrumental in spurring my original interest in antiquing, and where I had amassed such a large collection of photographs. While decorating our new house, I decided to hang some of the old photographs in my living room. I first displayed the photo of the young girl, decorating the frame with velvet ribbon in true Victorian style.

Twelve years later, in the summer of 1992, an elderly man knocked on my door. He introduced himself and told me that he was the great-grandson of the family that had lived on the farm from 1850 until 1957.

He said he had spent many summer vacations on the farm and just wanted to look around the old place. I enjoyed spending the afternoon with him, looking at the farm through his window into the past. When we were finished with the tour of the barns and the old slave house, I invited him inside for coffee.

As we sat talking, he noticed the picture of the young girl.

Much to my surprise, he asked, "Where did you get the picture of Great Aunt Sarah?"

"Aunt Sarah?" I repeated, confused. "I bought that picture at an auction twelve years ago. I have no idea who she is."

The old man said, "That's Aunt Sarah, all right. I have a photograph of her and I'm sure that's her."

He went on to tell me that Sarah had died of cholera

in 1855 at the age of eighteen. Then he added: "I think she died right here at home."

The old man later sent me a copy of his Aunt Sarah's obituary and a copy of the photograph he had mentioned.

Amazingly, it was indeed the same girl. According to her obituary, she died on a sofa in the living room, right near the spot where I had hung her picture and where it still hangs today. ❀

—SHIRLY GREER

The story is almost always the same, with little variation. It doesn't matter whether the setting is the Lower East Side of Manhattan or the Mattapan-Dorchester neighborhood in Boston. The place and the cast of characters might differ, but the story line never does. It is repeated countless times, in any city with a sizable population of Jews: A first-generation immigrant grandfather makes his way to the New Country and tries to integrate into the modern world, all the while clinging tenaciously to the customs and rituals of his religion. The second-generation son, disdainful of the traditions that have bound his father to the arcane practices, rebels and ditches most of the past, retaining only a few vestiges for sentiment's sake. The third-generation grandchild couldn't care less, and is totally ignorant of the heritage from whence he came.

Bobby Cohen* was a member of the third generation. His family lived in a suburb of Cleveland, far from the old neighborhood where his grandfather had originally settled in a suburb of big, spacious houses, wide manicured lawns, and big, shiny cars.

But something was beginning to happen to many members of the third generation; something was beginning to stir within them. Across the United States, in Jewish neighborhoods everywhere, a restlessness, an emptiness, a certain kind of void gnawed at the grandchildren. *Is this all there is to life?* they wondered, as they gazed at the houses, the lawns, and the cars that, no matter how impressive, expensive, and ostentatious, could not fill the gaping hole they felt inside. *There has to be more!*

Across the country, Bobby's personal yearning was being translated into a burgeoning communal movement. It was called the *baal teshuva* movement, the return of secular, assimilated Jews to their grassroots heritage—traditional Judaism. Organizations were founded and special schools established to meet the growing need. And in Cleveland, someone introduced Bobby to a group for teenagers called "NCSY"—National Council of Synagogue Youth.

One of the premises behind the organization's mandate was that the best way for kids to understand traditional Judaism was by *experiencing* it. "Experiential" became a favorite word used by "outreach workers"— Jewish men and women who volunteered their time and talents to introduce spiritual seekers to their heritage. Don't tell the kids about *Shabbat* (the Sabbath), the wisdom went; *show* it to them.

So, with the second generation's permission, teenagers

were taken away for a weekend to experience a typical Sabbath, complete with all the trimmings: prayer services, traditional *Shabbat* food, singing, dancing, classes, and just plain *shmoozing.* Many kids came away from these *Shabbatonim* (Sabbath weekends) galvanized toward a renewed interest in observing the traditions of their faith.

Bobby joined an NCSY group that held their *Shabbaton* (Sabbath weekend) on the other side of town, in an old Jewish neighborhood that was a relic of the past. Arrangements had been made for Bobby to stay with one of the few remaining Jewish families in the neighborhood, and after he unpacked and got dressed in his Sabbath gear, he made his way to the small synagogue where the NCSY *Shabbaton* was scheduled to take place.

The *shul* (synagogue) wasn't like any place of worship he had ever seen before. Like the houses, lawns, and cars they owned, the temple that the Cohens belonged to was large, shiny, and modern. This one, however, was small, musty, and worn. *Gee,* thought Bobby a little scornfully. *Couldn't they have found a better place?*

Still, once he settled into one of the seats—old-fashioned pews with their original congregants' names engraved on metal nameplates—he began to enjoy himself. The prayer service was beautiful, the singing joyous, and some of the rabbis even got up in the middle of the *davening* (praying) to dance. A rabbi explained the significance behind each prayer, and suddenly things that had seemed ridiculous to Bobby before now made a lot of sense. Right there in that room, everything was coming together for him. In that very seat, he felt a rush of emotion and connection the likes of which he had never truly experienced before. And it was then that Bobby's eyes were drawn to the metal nameplate on the arm of his chair. He had noticed it before, peripherally, but hadn't been interested enough to examine it closely. But as the evening became more meaningful to him, he wondered idly about the identity of the last person who had occupied his seat.

"Isidore Emanuel Nechemia Cohen," the nameplate read.

Bobby stared in disbelief. How many Isidore Emanuel Nechemia Cohens could there possibly be in Cleveland?

Not only was Bobby sitting in his grandfather's *shul,* but out of all the available pews, he had randomly chosen to sit in the exact same spot his grandfather had occupied decades before.

"Yes, I've come home tonight, *zayde* (grandfather)," he whispered to the ghost that hovered around him. "To you . . . to our heritage. And no, it can't be an accident that I'm back where you started. Thank you for sending me this sign." ❀

The restaurant was crowded and my wife and I waited at the bar until our table was called. A fire roared nearby and a Christmas tree stood in the corner, covered in small white lights. I ordered my wife a glass of wine and sipped at my draft beer while she lingered in the bathroom.

No doubt she was drying her eyes and reapplying a third coat of mascara, I thought bitterly, as I remembered the heated words and nasty barbs we had exchanged on the first leg of our trip from North Carolina to Florida.

We were going home to get a divorce. There was nothing pleasant about it. Neither of us was even trying anymore.

We had pulled over at the first nice restaurant we saw. Of course, we had passed 100 others along the way that either hadn't lived up to our expectations or weren't in my price range. The more our hunger grew, the more we blamed each other.

I grunted when the hostess told us that the wait would be over an hour. My wife sighed and disappeared into the ladies' room.

As I chewed on stale peanuts and ordered another beer, I watched the happy couples at and around the bar, basking in the firelight and looking forward to the New Year they had no doubt romantically greeted together.

My wife and I had spent the first day of the New Year storming around the house, dividing the CD collection and credit card bills. We had been married for four years, so there was a lot to go over.

I watched a young couple kiss, an older couple hold hands. I remembered a time, not too long ago, when my wife and I would have been right there with them. We would have lingered over cocktails at the bar on purpose, instead of just rushing in to find a table, eat, and get it over with.

I thought of the past year and its few ups and *many* downs. It had started with my job transfer, and things had gone downhill from there. My wife said good-bye to her fourth-grade students and we packed up the car and moved ten hours away. We had no friends, no family, and our first month's phone bill was enormous, as we tried to keep in touch with all the people we had left behind.

Ironically, my wife found a job where she quickly advanced, while my job — the reason for our relocation — turned out to be a big disappointment. Despite her satisfaction with her job, my wife sorely missed her family and former students, and I missed my old job. Nothing was working out quite right: the move had cost more than we expected; we had rented an expensive apartment we really didn't need; and there was nothing to do in our new town but eat and watch TV.

And fight.

Resentment grew with each passing month. But instead of talking to each other and sharing our problems as we had in the past, we turned to grumbling and grousing, fussing and fighting.

How could I tell her that I felt unfulfilled and defeated in my new job—the job that had caused her to uproot her whole life and follow her husband to a small town in the mountains of North Carolina? How could she tell me she hated going into work every morning and felt unfulfilled without being inside a classroom? In the end, neither of us told the other anything. When we spoke at all, it was to yell or accuse or snipe or bark.

My wife appeared at the bar, looking beautiful despite her puffy, cried-out eyes. I felt guilty at her tears—each drop was like a knife in my heart. There was a time in our life when the very thought of making her cry brought tears to my own eyes. But now each tear was like some stupid point on an invisible scoreboard.

As I watched her cross the room, I thought of my life without her and felt a lurch inside my stomach.

"How do I look?" she asked instinctively, and I had to laugh. It was a question she asked constantly. It was an inside joke we'd shared for years. Soon to be shared no more . . .

She thought I was laughing at her makeup, and with a sour expression on her face, she quickly downed her wine.

Our last name was finally called and we rushed through soup and rolls. Silver clinked on fancy plates as we chewed in silence. There was so much I wanted to say to her, but after all that we had decided, what was the point? Telling her I still loved her would only make our decision that much more difficult.

After ordering dinner I excused myself to go to the men's room, stopping on the way to place a reassuring hand on her shoulder. Not surprisingly, her body stiffened at my very touch.

While inside the men's room I heard the door burst open behind me and then the sound of water running. But my flushing couldn't cover the sound of a man sobbing.

When I emerged from the stall, I noticed a middle-aged man in a collared shirt and Dockers blubbering in front of the sink. He snuffled and snorted when he saw me, and I reached for paper towels and handed them to him in an unceremonious lump. He used them all and still the tears flowed. His face looked ruddy and flushed, and his washed-out eyes beseeched me to understand his predicament.

"I'm sorry," he choked. "It's just—the tree and the lights. I thought I was ready. I thought I could do all this. But then I heard the Christmas music and I just—it's the New Year already. Why do they have to keep playing the songs? I just couldn't do it. I'm sorry. I tried."

"Tried to do what?" I asked gently, hoping I wasn't prying. His pain seemed so intense, it was all I could do not to join him myself.

"Be . . . normal," he explained, blowing his nose. "My wife. You see . . . she died six weeks ago and I . . ."

"Six weeks!" I shouted, fear clutching my young heart. "I wouldn't be able to get out of bed if my wife had passed away six weeks ago." Despite our current state of affairs, I suddenly realized that this statement was all too true.

"I know," he nodded, "I know. But I managed to make it through Thanksgiving by drinking my way through a tropical cruise. I even managed to eat and sleep my way through Christmas. And . . . I thought I should be well by now.

"But Christmas was always her favorite holiday. I never stopped to listen to all of those silly Christmas songs until this very night. My appetizer came, my drinks, my salad. It all just sat there while I listened to the words. Over and over. Then I just started bawling. I'm sorry, you must think me a fool."

Just then the men's room door burst open, nearly knocking me to the ground. Two young men of college age rushed to surround the crying man. They wore expensive sweaters and grave expressions and called him "Dad." They asked if he was all right and turned their backs to me as they cleaned their father up in private.

The small room grew crowded and I left them to

their task. I wanted to ask the man how long he and his wife had been married, but by the age of his grown sons I assumed it was well beyond twenty years—or more.

I watched my wife's young face aglow in the candlelight, her fine hands curved around the heel of her wine glass. My legs felt leaden as I joined her at her seat, taking the chair beside her and pulling her into my arms just as the tears finally came.

"What's wrong?" she whispered into my hair as I clung to her chest. Her tone held no scorn, only bare and naked concern that her husband should feel pain.

After so many hateful words, so many petty barbs, I was *still* her husband.

"I'm sorry," I said, looking into her eyes.

Her tears bespoke her truest fears, and in seconds we were tripping all over each other's apologies. Relief overflowed our hearts as we spoke.

"I'll find a job back home," I sputtered. "I'll work two jobs, whatever it takes. I miss our family. I . . ."

"We'll both find jobs," she broke in. "You'll see. We'll be fine. Last year was horrible. This year will be fresh and . . ."

When our apologies and plans were spent, she held me close and whispered two words into my ear: "What happened?"

But how could I explain that in one quick bathroom visit I had lost—and then found—her all at the same time? ❀

—RUSTY FISCHER

When my grandparents died, I was unprepared and shocked. I berated myself for not saying "I love you" one last time. Afterwards, I was haunted by a sense of unfinished business, a lack of closure, the feeling that I hadn't quite gotten the job done.

Years later, I had two children of my own. I was so pleased to see my girls having the same wonderful relationship with their grandparents that I had had with mine. Yet, I was filled with fears. My father came from a family riddled with serious heart disease. I was concerned that his life would be cut short like those of his brothers who had already died. Like me, I wanted my girls to inherit wonderful memories of their grandparents. And, unlike my experience, I wanted to make sure they had no regrets. No "could haves," "should haves," or "would haves."

Fortunately, for my younger daughter, my father's final day on this earth was a gift. She will be blessed with the lifelong knowledge that, unlike her mother before her, she got the job done.

It was December 10, 1993. I had been baking for several

nights in preparation for Christmas. It was a Friday night, and I came home from work to make molasses cookies. When the dough was ready, I turned on the oven to preheat it, but something was wrong. I could not get the oven to work. It had worked all week long, but now it was malfunctioning. I was tired. It was cold outside, but I refused to waste the cookie dough and my own hard work. I called my mom and asked if I could use her oven instead. Of course, she said yes.

My husband and older daughter had gone to a basketball game. I couldn't leave my six-year-old alone, so I took her along to Grandma's house.

The cookies were already mixed, so all I had to do at my mother's house was preheat the oven and put the first dozen on the cookie sheet.

Dad was watching TV and reading the newspaper in the living room — two favorite activities that he did simultaneously. The first batch of cookies wasn't even baked when I heard a loud groan from the living room. Dad had fallen back in his chair. "Oh, my God!" I screamed.

I tried CPR with no success. I called 911. The paramedics were able to shock him and get a pulse. But when Dad got to the hospital, he was declared brain-dead.

The paramedics assured me that I had done all that I could. Dad had had a massive heart attack. No one could have saved him, they said. Now I began to worry about my younger daughter Katie and the horror she had witnessed. She had seen her beloved grandfather die right before her eyes.

We got through the wake and the funeral. My biggest concern was helping to heal Katie.

Months later, Katie and I were driving in the car. She was very quiet. Finally, in a small voice, she said, "You know the night Grandpa died, I was walking down the hall. I looked into the living room and he motioned for me to come to him."

"Did he say anything?" I asked.

"He said, 'Katie, I love you.'"

"And you?"

"I said, 'I love you too, Grandpa.'"

"What then?"

"I walked into the kitchen and a few minutes later you ran into the living room and screamed 'Oh, my God.'"

I began to cry. "Oh, Katie, do you realize how lucky you are?"

We talked about Grandpa for a long time. The experience of his death wasn't as traumatizing for Katie as I had thought. After all, she did get to tell her grandpa those three important, final words. *She* had gotten the job done—and all because my oven wouldn't work.

Oh, about that oven. A repairman came to look at it, eventually, and told me that it was in perfect working order. I had accidentally pushed a wrong button that made it appear to malfunction. Or, perhaps in this case, I had pushed the right button after all, on that fateful December evening. ❀

—CHERYL MALLON

*T*here are some things that never change, no matter *when* they happen or *where*. The country or continent is irrelevant; the time frame is inconsequential. They are universal experiences common to us all, scenarios that take place anywhere and everywhere in the world.

One universal tableau with which everyone is familiar is the scene of doting mothers on vacation snapping pictures of beloved offspring in any possible pose at every conceivable tourist site. Children groan in impatience; teenagers grimace; but most succumb to mothers' pleas and tender remonstrations. Later, these snapshots make their way into cherished family albums, for posterity and eternity.

Although the year was 1914 and the place was Strassburg, Germany, Elsie Kleiner was no different from the generations of mothers who had preceded her and those who would follow. She was on vacation at a beach resort with her only son and spent a goodly portion of the day hot on his trail, her trusty camera (much larger and cumbersome in those days) in hand. She was delighted to have caught him in several Kodak moments, building sand castles on the beach, skipping happily in front of a tranquil sea—and she was excited when she dropped off the film to be developed at a local store. She couldn't wait to see how the photos turned out.

Unfortunately, just at this precise time, fighting broke out between France and Germany, chaos erupted, and she had to hurriedly leave the city before picking up the film. She was grateful, of course, that she and her son were safe, but she always felt a twinge of regret about the pictures she would never see.

Two years later, Elsie was on vacation again—this time with her infant daughter, and this time in the city of Frankfurt, Germany. As before, she came equipped with her camera, prepared to do some serious picture taking—but she realized with a start that she had forgotten her film at home. So she stopped in at a local store and bought a roll. When she was done snapping pictures, she dropped the film off at the same store to be developed, and was told to return in three days (this was 1916, remember!). This time around, the war did not intrude upon her plans, and Elsie made it safely back to the store to retrieve her pictures.

The storekeeper handed her the envelope and she tore it open, eager to admire the results of her handiwork. Alas, a minor mishap—not a *war*, mind you, but a mishap nonetheless—had ruined her pictures again! The film was full of double exposures—other pictures super-imposed on the ones of her daughter—and Elsie realized with dismay that the storekeeper had sold her a used roll of film, not a new one!

"How could you do this?" she shrieked indignantly at the storekeeper. "You sold me an old roll of film that already had pictures taken on it! What kind of unscrupulous man are you?"

"Madam," the flustered man protested, "I had no idea it was an old roll of film. I myself bought it from another retailer. . . . I don't know how this happened. . . . I will gladly give you your money back."

But the man's embarrassed apologies were no longer necessary, for Elsie had taken a closer look at the double exposures and seen the familiar face of her *son* superimposed upon the images of her daughter.

Mysteriously, the same roll of film that Elsie had used in Strassburg two years earlier had found its way to Frankfurt and back into its rightful owner's hands. Elsie was now in possession of both the old photographs of her son and the new ones of her daughter, intertwined on a single roll of film. ✿

hen news spread all over Dale, Illinois, that a set of twins had been born to the Jones family, it seemed as though a cool breeze had blown through the town and stirred things up a little. Buildings and street signs that usually slouched stood tall and proud. Ladies lifted their skirts an inch over their boots and skip-walked to the grocer's. Gentlemen strutted like roosters in the streets, smiling and nodding at each other as if they were collectively responsible for the miraculous event. The year was 1903, and no one could recall the small town ever having hosted the birth of twins before.

It was no small task to select names for the girl and boy that would be satisfactory to both kith and kin. Friends suggested Virginia and Paul; Jane and John; Clara and Clare. They couldn't get together until J. C. Jones himself yelled, "I have it! We'll name them Tess and Ted." Now, every parent in Dale knew and appreciated "Tess and Ted" School Shoes, and nearly every boy and girl in Dale wore them. Mr. and Mrs. Jones loved the idea of naming their little ones after the solid and dependable footwear they themselves sold in their family store. The local newspaper announced the twins' christening with a photograph and the story of their naming them Tess and Ted Jones—a mighty nice bit of free advertising for J. C. Jones.

Perhaps because the town had so celebrated the birth of the twins, folks were simply devastated by the news of their deaths. Burying babies, while always a sad affair, was not uncommon at the time. But the little town of Dale completely shut down the day they laid the little ones out. Never had anything caused a crowd like the one that gathered at the Jones home just four months after Julia gave birth to the miracle babies.

One of the mourners was Ruth Leahy. Ruth was a childless neighbor who often took in one or two of the older Jones children when Mrs. Jones was up to her ankles in dirty dungarees or canning her famous strawberry rhubarb preserves. That very day, Ruth had quietly taken it upon herself to keep an eye on the Jones brood while Julia and J. C. received their guests. When the crowd thinned, she approached the caskets for the first time and touched her gloved hand to her mouth to mask her trembling. She laid her hand on little Ted's chest to give him an Irish blessing she was sure would help him fly right past purgatory and straight to heaven. What she hadn't expected was to feel the subtle rise and fall of a sleeping child. She looked at the boy's body lying so still, but again beneath her hand, the tiny chest filled weakly with air—then expelled it with equal effort.

Ruth was then able to call out, "The boy . . . alive . . . Doc . . ." before dropping into the nearest chair for a brief faint. The doctor was among the remaining visitors, and he responded first to Mrs. Leahy sprawled pale in the chair. When it became clearer what Ruth was suggesting, Doc examined the baby. His gray brows pointed fiercely at the bridge of his nose and, with great authority, he lifted the boy over his head and shook him. The boy was indeed breathing, and strongly enough then that those nearby heard a sweet infant coo before Ted Jones fell back asleep.

The room exploded with chaos and the crowd parted so that J. C. and Julia could reach their son. Amidst the uproar, Doc examined the baby girl. But there would be only one miracle that day. Ted bid farewell to the sister he knew so briefly, but the Joneses reclaimed the son they thought they had lost.

I never met Ted Jones; he died well before I was born. But the story of his "rebirth" always intrigued me. Nor have I met Ruth Leahy—a pseudonym I created to replace the unknown person who discovered baby Ted was alive. Unfortunately, her name has been lost to history. I feel that she, whoever she really was, must have been a guardian angel. Ted Jones, you see, was my grandfather. I owe my life—and the lives of my own children—to "Ruth Leahy." ❀

—LISA NAEGER SHEA

*W*hat are the odds that the wrong number will get the right party?

Theresa Wilson had been a toddler of three when her parents divorced, and her mother had disappeared from her life together with her siblings. Theresa's mother, considered emotionally unstable, had been legally denied both custody and visitation rights, and consequently her Theresa never saw her again.

But all her young life, Theresa wondered about the mother she barely knew. Her dad never spoke of her, but Theresa yearned to meet her.

At the tender age of sixteen, she became determined to find her mother, no matter what. The odds were daunting—but whoever heard of daunting odds fazing a *teenager?*

Theresa had two clues in her possession: the first was her mother's maiden name; the second was her last-known whereabouts. The city her mother had last been known to live in wasn't large—Port Richey, Florida—but her maiden name was somewhat of a more formidable challenge: James. *Well, how many Jameses could there be in one small city?* Theresa thought. As it turned out, there were thirty-one.

"Are you *sure* you want all thirty-one numbers?" the operator from directory assistance asked dubiously.

"Please," Theresa begged, "I'm trying to find my mother!"

Theresa was persistent. She called twenty-five James homes, asking each time if anyone there knew of her mother and/or had ever heard of her. Each time the answer was no. But when Theresa dialed the twenty-sixth number, she made a mistake.

Theresa had copied the number down incorrectly, reversing two of the last four digits. She dialed 3916 instead of 3196.

"Does Kathy James live here?" Theresa's trembling voice asked the person who picked up the phone, unaware that she had not reached the James residence, but the Marcum home instead.

"She doesn't live here, but I do happen to know her," answered Joan Marcum, who had been a neighbor of the Jameses several years before. "I think I have the number somewhere. Hold on a minute and I'll get it for you."

"We were reunited by a sheer miracle," Theresa's mother, Kathy Hoppe, later told reporters. "The odds of this happening are one in a million. I'm still in a state of shock that Theresa found me through a wrong number."

When Kathy vanished from Theresa's life, she had

been an undiagnosed manic-depressive. Later, she underwent treatment for her condition and today she takes medication for the disorder.

"But no matter what I was going through all those years," Kathy said, "I never stopped loving—or thinking about—my kids." ❀

*L*oving and nurturing mean different things to different people, but when it comes to the archetypal Jewish mother, there is really only one thing that spells love, and the word is F-O-O-D.

Jewish mothers have reportedly been seen dashing determinedly after recalcitrant young eaters, brandishing spoons filled with food—their weapon of choice. The tables they set groan under the sheer weight of all the food laid upon them, and the moment a visitor sets foot into a Jewish home, he/she is alternately invited, cajoled, beseeched, and inexorably commanded to "eat a little something; it's good for you."

For millennia, Jewish mothers have regarded food as the ultimate panacea, the paramount and supreme cure-all for whatever ails both body and spirit. You have a few sniffles, *mamela?* Let me give you some chicken soup. *Nebech* (you poor soul), you just broke your engagement? Have a piece of my sponge cake, guaranteed to banish the blues.

Considering the intricate connection that exists between Jews and food—and the notoriety enjoyed by

Jewish mothers worldwide for supplying it in abundance—it was no wonder that when Brooklynite Suri Feldman told her mother that she was going on a school trip to a Massachusetts state park, the first thing her mother said was, "You'll need a lot of sandwiches!"

"Ma, please," Suri groaned. "One is enough."

"One?" her mother shrieked. "For a whole day? Are you *meshuga* (crazy)? You'll starve!"

On the day of the trip, Suri lugged a huge shopping bag brimming with sandwiches, drinks, and snacks onto the charter bus. She would have been mortified by her excessive supplies if her classmates hadn't been dragging, heaving, and buckling under similar weights of their own.

The girls warily eyed each other's stockpiles and then laughed. Each mother had outdone the others; there was enough food on the bus to feed an army. "How are we supposed to *shlep* this stuff on a hike, anyway?" one grumbled. "Maybe we'll leave the bags on the bus and come back in the middle of the day to eat," another hazarded a guess.

But when the bus arrived at the state park, the girls were instructed to take their shopping bags along with them. "It doesn't make sense to hike back and forth to the bus," one teacher explained. "We'll take our lunches along with us and eat together in the forest. Anyway, it'll be more fun."

"Fun?" one girl moaned. "Has she taken a look at what our mothers packed?"

"Don't worry," Suri reassured the six girls she was walking with. "You know I'm blessed with super strength. I'll carry your bags for you when you get tired."

As they hiked over hills and difficult trails, the other girls—city dwellers more used to excursions to the mall than treks in the woods—began to tire and lag behind Suri. They were straining under the pressure of the sacks of food they were hauling.

"Give me your shopping bags," Suri urged her friends. "Really, it's OK. I can manage."

With their loads removed, the girls' pace quickened. Suri, on the other hand, now bearing the brunt of seven Jewish mothers' conceptions of what constitutes enough food for a day trip, began to slow down. Soon her friends were out of range—but none of them realized that Suri was not faithfully trudging behind until a significant amount of time had elapsed.

"Where's Suri?" one suddenly said, turning around to glance backward.

At the outset of the hike, the school had separated into different groups, and it took Suri's friends a while to ascertain that Suri was not hiking with any of the other groups. It was only then that they approached the teacher in charge and sounded the alarm.

Suri Feldman made national headlines as the thirteen-year-old Hasidic girl who disappeared in a Massachusetts forest on May 9, 1994. About two weeks earlier, another teenage girl had gotten lost in a nearby stretch of woods and had later been found dead. As teams of volunteers from all over the East Coast converged on the state park to search for Suri, police privately shared their fears that the same fate might await her.

The fears deepened as three days passed without Suri being found. How could a Hasidic girl—ignorant of basic survival skills and lacking even the street smarts of inner-city kids—survive two nights and three days, alone, in a forest?

Suri was reciting her afternoon prayers when she heard the rescue workers shout her name. Although the searchers were reassured by Suri's spirited responses and robust color, they nonetheless rushed her to the hospital, convinced that she had to be suffering from dehydration and shock. In the hysteria that had ensued after Suri had disappeared, her classmates had forgotten the bags of food she had generously offered to carry. And it was precisely those reserves that—together with the grace of God and people's prayers from all over the world—helped keep her alive.

One intrepid newspaper reporter, however, seeking a new angle that he could sensationalize, attempted to turn the story into a scandal. He smelled something fishy, he said. Why would a young girl have so much food in her possession? Was she perhaps trying to "run away from home"? After doing a bit more research, the reporter backed down with both an apology and a retraction.

He had made a mistake, he later admitted. He had

assumed that the teenage girl's home, which overflowed with thirteen children, had proven unbearable for her. As an outsider to the Hasidic community, the reporter had not understood that such a home could be filled with as much love and light, warmth, and devotion as homes that averaged the typical American two children.

How could he have known that it was in precisely such a home that the loving hands of her tender mother—as well as those of several other mothers—had provided for her in her time of need. Together with God who had shielded her, it was a mother's love that had kept Suri safe during her three-day ordeal—a blessing that would endure for the rest of her life. ✿

When a Los Angeles police officer pulled a Northridge man over for having an expired license plate in September 1998, he got more than he bargained for during the exchange that followed.

No, the irate motorist didn't pull out a gun to wave at the cop, nor did he shout profanities and epithets. Instead of being violent and abusive, he was polite and respectful. But he still wanted out of the ticket, so he tried a ploy that gave the officer the shock of his life.

The motorist squinted at the cop's name tag and noticed that it coincidentally bore the same last name as his own: Benitez. *Hmm,* he thought, *it's a long shot—there are certainly a lot of Benitezes around. But at least maybe I can get out of the ticket. It's certainly worth a try.*

So the motorist flashed the cop his most winning smile and asked casually: "Is your first name Kelly by any chance?"

When the policeman answered yes, the motorist's jaw dropped. He looked the cop squarely in the eye, leaped from his car, tossed his arms around him, and exclaimed,

"And my name is Paul Benitez. I believe that I'm your long-lost dad!"

And, indeed, he was.

The two had been searching for one another for years until fate, luck—or was it something else?—brought them together in one traffic-stopping reunion.

Paul Benitez, the forty-nine-year-old father, had been ripped by tremendous remorse and guilt for years over having abandoned his infant child, Kelly, and leaving him fatherless. Several months after Kelly's birth, his father had left Los Angeles for a tour of duty in the army and had never returned to his family.

"The sixties were a difficult time for young people, including myself," Paul said ruefully, recalling his irresponsible act with regret. Kelly, now twenty-nine, had been raised by his maternal grandparents, who, according to Paul, "did a great job."

"What are the odds of a police offer pulling over the father he hasn't seen in twenty-nine years?" Kelly Benitez remarked at a news conference later that month. "It's eerie."

Asked by reporters if there was a moral to the story, Paul at first joked: "Take care of your registration tag!" Then, getting more serious, he said, "Hey, I'm kidding. There definitely is a moral to this story and here it is.

"If there's someone out there you're looking for, don't give up!"

Meanwhile, he's renewed his registration, which was "just a little bit expired" after all. ❀

*C*an it already be ten years since our oldest son was born? We just celebrated our youngest son's birthday, and now his older brother's birthday party is just around the bend.

Birthdays never meant much to my husband or myself until we became parents ourselves. The miraculous arrival of longed-for children into our home when we were well into our forties changed our perspective. Now these special days have taken on new significance and are laden with meaning. To me, it is clear that nothing less than divine orchestration brought these children into our lives, and I bless the day they both arrived.

It was an overcast early spring morning in 1990 when my husband John and I were awakened by a 6:00 A.M. phone call.

"It's a boy!" rang the excited voice of the biological grandmother of the child, announcing the arrival of the baby we had been waiting for since autumn.

"He's beautiful," she continued.

Although it was a wet and dreary morning, we took

little notice of the weather. It seemed to us as if the sun had broken through the clouds, even though it still remained dark outside. My husband and I couldn't get to the hospital fast enough. I was the first to hold the baby. *You're meant to be my son,* I thought tenderly. Just as his grandmother had said, the baby was indeed beautiful. And soon to be ours. Words couldn't express how I felt at that moment.

We had held many discussions with the young woman who was giving up her son for adoption, but they had always been over the telephone, never in person. Now we were meeting the birth mother for the first time, and I was delighted to see that her hair and eye color matched mine. John, in turn, was thrilled to be told by the hospital nurse, "Oh, the baby looks like *you!*" We both felt so grateful then to God, to our son's birth mother, and to all those involved who had made this milestone event in our lives happen.

"You can take the baby home in two days," the social worker informed us. The weeks that followed brimmed with wonder, excitement, and brand-new experiences — experiences we had begun to believe would never be ours to share.

During the early years of our marriage, we realized that the prospects of my becoming pregnant were small, due to my mature age. The odds were further complicated by the fact that I had a medical condition called endometriosis. This chronic, often painful disease occurs when some of the tissue that lines the uterus grows in abnormal locations. It is a component that underlies many cases of infertility, and was believed to be a contributing factor to mine.

By my early forties, I had already undergone several surgeries that brought some physical relief, but little hope of having children. My doctor's prognosis was that pregnancy was "not utterly impossible, but extremely improbable."

"You might wish to consider adoption," she suggested one day with genuine concern in her voice. She gave us all the information about an upcoming seminar on adoption, sponsored by RESOLVE, a national self-help organization that provides extensive counseling for couples struggling with infertility. Although John and I hadn't seriously contemplated adoption before, we attended the meeting and became enthused by the possibilities this new direction offered us. Soon we were making the rounds of adoption agencies, even though we were well above the age limit for an agency adoption.

"Explore all your options," one adoption service strongly advised.

We retained an attorney who specialized in private, independent adoption. We completed and successfully fulfilled all the criteria required for private adoption, including a criminal investigation and a three-month study of our home by a social service agency. But this avenue, too, proved unproductive. A full year and a half elapsed, but nothing changed. Our prospects seemed as bleak as they had been eighteen months before.

I couldn't just sit and wait. I tried to be proactive and resourceful. Since I worked in a hospital and had many contacts there, I networked as much as I could. I was surprised to discover that I was far less timid than I had expected myself to be: I was determined to get the word out, to let as many people as possible know of our desire to adopt. Despite our many disappointments, I was still hopeful.

One afternoon, I had a strong impulse to call the doctor who had originally suggested adoption. I hadn't spoken to her for a long time, but I suddenly felt that she might be able to provide me with further help. I could not explain why her name sprang to my mind at the time, but I followed my instincts.

"The doctor has relocated and is now practicing in another part of the state," the receptionist told me. This didn't deter me a bit. I asked for the doctor's new number and dialed it immediately. Having come this far, I was unwilling to stop now.

"The doctor is with a new patient," I was informed by her assistant. "She might not be able to get back to you today." Undeterred, I left my name and telephone number.

My former gynecologist returned my call later that evening. I explained why I was contacting her and asked if she knew of anyone seeking a home for a newborn baby.

"I don't right now, but I'll let you know if I can help," she promised.

I was elated that I had established another potential source for an independent adoption. *But will any of these attempts prove successful?* I wondered.

The answer to this question came ten days later when my former gynecologist gave me a call. "Jeanne, I have a baby for you. The very afternoon you called, I was in the middle of examining a distraught young woman who had come to my office accompanied by her mother. Later tests confirmed my suspicions: She was pregnant.

"The young woman felt that she would be unable to provide her baby with a good life. For several days, she agonized, but she finally made the decision to give her child up for adoption. I told her about you, and she wants you to be the one to raise this child."

"This is too good to be true," I said.

My former physician remarked that my timing had been impeccable. "What a remarkable coincidence," she said, "that you called at the exact time that I was administering the pregnancy test to my patient." ❀

—JEANNE P. DAVIS

I always regarded both of my parents with a mixture of awe and admiration. My perceptions of my mother and father as special human beings—constantly engaged in charity and good works—never wavered, even when I entered the turbulent teenage years. The consequences of this perspective were enormous: My confidence in my parents' intrinsic goodness—that they were saintly and righteous people— would reverberate throughout my life in ways I could never have envisioned.

I grew up in prewar Europe—in a Hungarian city called Sighet—just before Hitler cast his long shadow over my people. Unlike many of the impoverished townspeople, my father, Yosef Moshe Zicherman, was an affluent businessman who owned a small department store, and he was considered a distinguished leader of the local Jewish population. Intensely involved in communal affairs, my father anonymously supplied widows, orphans, and poor families with food, money, and wood (for fuel) throughout their lives. Most of them would never learn the identity of their mysterious benefactor.

In 1940, when I was eighteen years old, my father suddenly fell ill with severe intestinal pains. Although his doctor wasn't unduly alarmed by my father's condition, he nonetheless recommended surgery as the only viable treatment. Since the operation was supposed to be routine and uneventful, I was the only one dispatched to accompany my father to the local hospital where the surgery had been scheduled. The doctor assured my mother that the operation was not life-threatening and that she could safely stay home.

We were running late, but my father's pace was slow and unhurried. Once inside the hospital lobby, my father paused and pulled out a comb. He started grooming himself carefully. I stared in disbelief. My father was not a vain man, and the surgeon was waiting. *What was he doing?*

"*Tatta* (father)," I urged, "we must hurry."

My father's look was enigmatic. Instead of heading in the direction of the surgical department, he led me instead toward the business office, and, in the same leisurely manner as before, lowered himself into a chair in the reception area. I was thoroughly nonplussed.

"*Tatta,*" I asked, bewildered, "what are you doing?" Ignoring my question, he began to delineate for me in laborious detail the names of various people to whom he owed money. "I owe Mr. Schwartz 2,000 *pecros*," he began. "I owe Mr. Hyman 5,000, Mr. Rabinowitz 4,000 . . ."

"*Tatta!*" I screamed. "Why are you telling me this?

You shouldn't concern yourself with these matters right now. You'll pay your debts after the operation."

Once again disregarding my comments, he continued his inventory. Then he paused and said, "Go call your brothers to leave yeshiva and come to the hospital right away."

I gazed at my father dumbfounded, not wishing to confront the implication of his remark. Earlier that day, my father had mentioned to me that his intestinal pains had disappeared, and that he didn't even know whether the operation was still necessary. His color was robust and he appeared strong. And he was only fifty-two years old. Why was he behaving as if he were a man putting his affairs in order—like a man about to die?

"*Tatta*, I don't understand. What is going on?"

"Don't let your mother cry," he commanded sternly.

I became panic-stricken, and tears stung my eyes. My father was acting *so* strangely.

Suddenly, he clutched me to him, hugged me hard, and started showering me with blessings. He said many things to me that day, but the one that remained with me was the particular phrase that he kept repeating over and over again.

"*Mein kind* (my child), I promise you, you will marry one day, and you will have wonderful and religious children."

Then he released his grip on me, slumped forward and collapsed in his chair. As I screamed for help, a nurse rushed to my father's side and felt for his pulse.

"He's dead," she pronounced grimly.

I swooned and fainted on the floor.

At my father's funeral—overflowing with the multitudes who came to pay their last respects to one of the most beloved figures in town—there were five women, strangers, whom I didn't know and had never seen before. What made their appearance at my father's funeral all the more incongruous was their conspicuous grief. Their faces were tear-streaked, and their voices—shrill with despair—rose up over the cries of the other mourners.

"*Tatta*," they shrieked, "who will bring us wood for the winter, matzos for *Pesach*, fish for *Shabbos*?" I looked at them in shock. I felt as if the tragedy of my father's death was causing me to hallucinate. Who were these women, and why were they calling my father their *Tatta*?

The *Sigheter Rebbe* (Rabbi of Sighet), seeing the apparent pain and confusion on my face, later disclosed to me one of my father's many secrets—a secret he had confided only to him: These women were young widows, and my father had single-handedly taken it upon himself to support their families. No one had known of this aspect of my father's charity work except for the widows themselves, and the Rebbe. The disclosure of this secret only reaffirmed my long-standing conviction that my father was a *tzaddik* (a saint).

Hungary was invaded by the Nazis in 1944, and my mother and I became ensnared in Hitler's web. We were herded like animals into crowded cattle cars and forced to live under the most inhumane circumstances, without food, water, or toilet facilities. In those cattle cars, which transported us to Auschwitz, we had our first introduction to the bestiality that would become our "normal" way of life in the camps.

As the train ground to a halt and we spilled out onto the tracks, havoc ensued. Families that had clung tightly together in the trains were brutally separated—before there was even time for a last kiss, a final farewell. Children were torn from their mothers' arms, married couples were split apart, siblings were sent different ways. I watched in terror as a guard dragged my mother away from me and placed her in a group of older women.

In the midst of the chaos, a young concentration camp inmate whose job it was to unload the dead bodies from the cattle cars sidled up to me. He looked at my long, flowing locks of golden hair and whispered to me: "Do you know what the Nazis do to young women like you? They do all kinds of horrible things to them. They rape them, and torture them, and then when they're finished with them, they throw them into the furnaces." He nodded in the direction of my mother. "I don't know whose fate is worse—yours or hers. Girls like you get a temporary reprieve for days, weeks, even months—but older people like your mother are thrown into the furnaces upon arrival."

"In that case, I don't want to live," I said fiercely. "I

want to stay with my mother. If she dies, I want to die, too . . . Can you help me?" I pleaded with the boy.

"I'll help you," he said.

Amidst the confusion that still reigned, the boy motioned to me to dart over to the group where my mother stood and showed me how to make myself as inconspicuous as possible. Still, despite my best attempts, I couldn't blend in with the older women. My youth shone out in stark contrast. As soon as the notorious Mengele stepped out of the hut where he worked to survey the next fodder for the furnaces, his steely gaze came to rest on me straightaway. He waved his baton at me, and screamed: "You! Come here! This side!"

"I'll be back," I promised my mother.

As soon as Mengele had his back turned for a fraction of a second, I bolted back to my mother's group. But Mengele spied me again, and pinioned me with his scrutiny once more. This time he personally hauled me away from the older women and planted me firmly in the group with the young girls. Then he raised his baton and smacked me squarely in the face.

I reeled from the blow, but my determination was still strong. The young boy, still trying to help me orchestrate my return to my mother, pantomimed patience to me from across the divide that separated us. Risking his life, he caused a momentary uproar to distract Mengele and aid me, and for the third time, I was able to race back to my mother's side.

"Don't worry," I reassured her. "I won't leave you. I want to be wherever you are. I want to go wherever you go, even if it's into the crematorium. Without you I don't want to live."

My mother looked at me with great sadness and gently said: "*Mein kind,* please go back to the other side. And I promise you: you will marry, and you will have wonderful, religious children."

I stubbornly shook my head *no*. No, I would not leave my mother's side. No, I would not return to the younger group; without her, life was not worth living. But my fate was not mine to decide. For the third and final time, Mengele spied me, strode over to where I stood, and clubbed me harshly. He beat me so savagely, in fact, that darkness overcame me, and I blacked out completely.

When I regained consciousness, I found myself in a dark hut, pinned underneath a pile of bodies, most of them motionless, a few still writhing. I saw a young girl—barely conscious—twist and thrash nearby, and I dragged myself out of the hut, pulling her out with me. A guard suddenly appeared and barked "Don't move!" A bullet rang out. The young girl whom I had tried to save was dead.

When the guard disappeared from view, I crept along the ground toward the nearest barracks and crawled in. There I found not one but five close friends from Sighet who screamed: "Chaya Ruchel, you're alive!" They gave me their own meager portions of coffee and water and revived me. It was then that consciousness dawned, and I realized that my mother must have been taken to the crematorium. In the traditional gesture of mourning, I ripped the fabric of the collar of my dress, but my friends didn't understand the significance of my action. They assumed that in the first few hours of concentration camp, I had gone stark, raving mad.

"Stay with us," they begged, "we'll take care of you."

And so, we became each other's family, and kept one another alive. On three separate occasions, we were called for final selection, but on all three occasions we were granted a last-minute reprieve. Each time, as we filed toward the crematorium, reciting psalms and preparing for death, we would suddenly be halted in our tracks by Mengele, who would tell the guards that the quota for the day was "filled"; there was simply no more room in the gas chambers for any more bodies. Sometimes we would be only a few yards away from the crematorium door when Mengele would suddenly revoke our certain death sentence. This scenario was repeated three times.

One night, I had a strange dream. In the dream, my father appeared to me and said in a loud and clear voice: "Chaya Ruchele, be sure that you are the first one in line for selection tomorrow morning."

When I woke up, I roused my friends and recounted the cryptic dream. They looked at me askance as I told them what my father had commanded me to do.

I understood their skepticism: it was a strange and incongruous dream. After all, who *volunteers* for selection?

Since the day they had first found me, my friends and I had done everything together, and we were as one. But as much as they loved me, they certainly weren't going to volunteer for a clear and obvious death.

"My friends," I said, "you can do whatever you want tomorrow, but my holy father seems to miss me in Heaven and wants me there with him, so I am going to do his bidding."

I said my good-byes to them, and we all cried. In the morning, I was the first in line, and Mengele seemed shocked to find me there, ready and waiting. Suddenly, I heard a commotion behind me, and was surprised to find all five of my friends lined up behind me.

"What are you doing here?" I stammered in disbelief.

"We talked about your dream this morning," one of my friends said. "We spoke about your father and how we remembered him as being special and how in fact everyone in Sighet knew him as a holy man. We decided that if he told you to volunteer for selection, we're doing it too! We're holding on to your coattails, Chaya Ruchel!" With his baton, Mengele waved us in the direction of the crematorium, and we were stripped naked before we entered the building labeled "Showers." Long ago we had learned that the sign was only a ruse; gas flowed out of the showerheads, not water. The doors opened, we filed in, we recited the *Shema* (last prayer before certain death), we stood under the showerheads, and we waited for death. But to our utter stupefaction and joy, it was water that came pouring out of the showerheads—water, not gas. We yelled, "It's water! It's water!" And we jumped and screamed in shock and disbelief, knowing that some miracle had been wrought, and that our death sentence had once again been suspended.

Later, we would learn that the German city of Breslau had just been bombed and was now almost completely destroyed. The Germans needed laborers—fast—to clean up and rebuild the city. That morning, we had been sure we would be gassed, but we were taken to a work camp in Breslau instead. And there we stayed, together, alive, until the end of the war, when we were liberated.

I met and married my husband in a DP (displaced persons) camp in Germany in 1949, and, like other survivors, we began to rebuild our shattered lives. And soon I learned that I was pregnant.

Although my pregnancy gave me cause for great joy, the labor and delivery were physically harrowing experiences. I am a very small woman, but the baby was huge. After an exceedingly difficult labor, the doctor had to resort to a caesarean section. Despite this last-minute recourse, the baby was born dead, and I almost died myself.

"You can't have any more children," the doctor warned. "Another delivery will kill you. Even C-sections are too dangerous for your frail health."

I couldn't accept his pronouncement as true; I didn't

want to believe that I wouldn't be able to have children. I made the rounds of many specialists, hoping that at least one of them would retract my first doctor's opinion, offering me a reprieve from the death of all my hopes and dreams. But not a single one would tell me the words I longed to hear. After each successive examination, every single one of them echoed the previous doctor's advice: "Don't dare get pregnant again."

I went to all of these well-meaning doctors for counsel, but it didn't necessarily follow that I heeded their advice. Call me feisty, call me strong-willed, call me a woman with a mind of her own. Five months later, I was pregnant again.

The second time around, caesarean section was even more problematic than the first. The scenarios were almost identical, with one critical exception. Once again, I almost died. But this time, the baby—a big boy weighing over eleven pounds—lived.

"You are very, very lucky that you survived this time," my doctor angrily admonished me. "But don't you dare think of conceiving again! You must go on birth control immediately. Will you finally listen to me?"

Half a year later, I was pregnant again.

For obvious reasons, I was reluctant to make an appointment with my regular obstetrician and kept on putting it off. But when I began experiencing excruciating back pain, I had no alternative but to pay him a visit.

"What you have done? What have you done?" he

screamed at me as soon as he learned my condition. "I told you not to get pregnant! You must have an abortion or you'll die!"

Once again, I made the rounds of various specialists and once again all concurred with the first doctor's determination. Then, to compound matters, my brother, a very pious man, got involved. "You have to be a mother to the son you already have," he cried, pleading that I have the abortion. He, in turn, consulted with three different rabbis—all great sages—and they too unanimously agreed that an abortion was religiously acceptable when a mother's life was at genuine risk.

Since the consensus of both the rabbis and the doctors was exactly the same, I was forced to yield to my husband, to my brother, and to the powers that be, and I unwillingly agreed to have the pregnancy terminated.

The night before the abortion, my sleep was restless and tormented.

All night long, two vivid memories—two distinct scenes—were repeatedly enacted in my head, like a film that is rewound and replayed, over and over again.

First, I remembered clearly, as if it had happened yesterday, how my father had clutched me to him before his death and said: "Chaya Ruchele, I promise that you will marry and you will have wonderful, religious children."

Children, my father had said, not *child*. Plural, not singular.

And then I remembered how, right before her own

death, my mother had repeated, almost word for word, the same blessing as my father. "Chaya Ruchele, go back to the other side. You will live, you will marry, and you will have wonderful, religious children."

Children, she had said, not *child*. Plural, not singular. How could both my parents be wrong?

Throughout the night, I thought about my dear mother and father, how much they had loved me, how much they had sacrificed for me, and how they had both tried to save my life. Both saintly, both pious, both holy. And both had, separately and unknowingly, given me the exact same blessing: *children*.

But if I had the abortion tomorrow, I would have only one child. How could I subvert their blessings? And how much did I believe in the power of their words, their love?

The next morning, I decided: *I can't do it, I can't live with myself, I can't have an abortion.* So I tiptoed through the house while my husband slept, grabbed my infant son, and fled to a friend's house.

"I had a fight with my husband, and I want to teach him a lesson," I told her. "Can I stay?"

I knew that if I told my friend the truth about the impending abortion and she learned that my life was in peril, she would send me packing back to my husband, to the hospital, to the abortion. So, for the first time in my life, I prevaricated, and consequently stayed in her home until four o'clock in the afternoon, when I assumed it was now safe for me to return home.

As I opened the door nervously, I found my household in an uproar. My husband and brother were crying and the police had been summoned. I turned to my husband and said: "I know that you're angry with me, and you can do with me whatever you want, but my mother and father both promised me *kinder* (children), not *ein kind* (one child), and I believe in the power of their blessing. I cannot and will not throw away the child that is growing inside of me."

Now my husband and brother surrendered to *me*. My pregnancy was terrible, and the prognosis remained poor, but I had tremendous faith in my parents' blessing and, of course, in God.

No one else around me shared my hope or trust. When the women of the DP camp would pass me by, they would either avert their eyes or look at me with great pity, certain that I was going to die.

But I knew differently. Not once in their lifetimes had my parents ever let me down. "Don't worry," I told my husband with absolute confidence. "I will have a daughter and your deceased mother of blessed memory will have a namesake."

On the morning of *Tisha B'av* (the fast day that commemorates the destruction of the Temple), I was wheeled into the delivery room for my caesarean, and through the haze of anesthesia finally heard the doctor say: "It's a girl!"

As both my parents promised, my son and daughter have grown up to be wonderful and religious children, and between them have given me twenty grandchildren, all of whom follow the path of their forefathers.

"Honor your mother and father so that your days may be lengthened," the Ten Commandments say. In this case, it was not only my own life that was saved because of my love and respect for my parents, but my children's and grandchildren's as well. Three generations are alive today because I took that commandment seriously and incorporated it into every aspect of my life. ❀

— ROSA RUCHEL HERSKOVITZ

*I*n March 1989, my mother died of cancer following surgery to remove a tumor. We hadn't even known she had cancer until the surgery, and then she died eleven days later. It was a shock to all of us.

On June 23, 1990, on what would have been her seventy-third birthday, I was alone in my house, getting ready to go out for the evening. My husband was out back doing yardwork. Since it was summer, all of the windows were open. I was startled by the sound of a phone being dialed on a speakerphone; I heard the tones as each number was pressed.

The first time I heard the noise, I barely paid attention. Then the phone was dialed a second time and I thought, *How very odd that I can hear my neighbors dialing their phones. All these years—even summertime when the windows are wide open—I've never been able to hear them dial their phones before.* But when I heard the phone being dialed a third time, I was spooked. I realized that the clear and unmistakable sounds of buttons being punched out on a touch-tone speakerphone were not coming from my neighbor's house at all, but rather, mysteriously, from mine.

This is weird, I thought. I looked out the window to check on my husband and saw him still stationed in the yard, diligently weeding away. *No one else is in the house but me. Who could be using the phone?*

I headed toward my husband's empty office — the source of those shrill speakerphone noises — and saw that the red light on his phone was on. It lit up whenever it was in use.

I picked up the phone and the voice of my father came on the line, asking with sharp annoyance, "Who are you? Why do you keep calling me and not saying anything?"

Totally perplexed, I said, "Daddy, what are you doing on my phone?"

"What do you mean, what am I doing on your phone?" he bellowed. "What are *you* doing — are you calling me or what?"

"Daddy!" I shouted in exasperation. "I didn't call you. Didn't you call me?"

It was then that I realized that my phone had been dialing his number — not once, not twice, but three separate times. My father's phone number was not on speed dial, since this was my husband's business phone and he did not have my father's number programmed on it. As much as I would have liked to, I could not chalk up the incident to a phone glitch or an operating malfunction. And there was not a single other soul in the house at the time.

Who had made that call?

Both my father and I reached the same conclusion at the same time. The anonymous dialer could be one person and one person only—my mom.

After I hung up the phone, I went back to my bedroom and picked up the framed photograph I keep near my bed. I addressed the photo.

"OK, Mother," I laughed, "I'm sorry I didn't wish you a happy birthday before."

I'm convinced that the "mysterious caller" kept persistently dialing until I went to investigate. Once I wished my mother a "Happy Birthday" out loud, the dialing abruptly stopped, and the mysterious "glitch" never occurred again. ❀

—JANET WHITE SPERBER

What would *you* do if you stumbled upon a stray bullet in a city park? Pick it up, inspect it, and toss it back on the ground where you originally found it? Dispose of it in the nearest trash can? Shudder at the mere sight of it and kick it out of your way as you proceed on your walk?

Most people would do one of the above, right? It's not as if a stray bullet is a cache of valuables or someone's lost wallet, right? Finding a bullet in one's neighborhood park may be unsettling, but it's certainly not an earthshaking event. Or is it?

Earl Kloth, a homeless man who lived in Racine, Wisconsin, was foraging in a city park one day when he unearthed the bullet. As far as he could tell, it had not been used, but was, in common parlance, "a live one."

Earl didn't shrug his shoulders in indifference; he didn't think it was an inconsequential find. Rather, he shuddered with the responsibility of having uncovered such a potentially dangerous item. What if it was indeed a live bullet, and not a used one? What if it got into the wrong hands? If he left it on the ground where he had found it, what might happen if the next person to encounter it was a child? One who had a daddy with guns in his closet?

Earl felt that he couldn't take a chance and just leave it there. Perhaps the next person who would retrieve it would be less scrupulous than he. So he brought the bullet to the Racine Presbyterian Church (which doubles as a homeless shelter on Sunday nights) and turned it over to the officials in charge. He assumed that he was doing his duty as a good citizen, and that that would be the end of it.

As a man who had been homeless most of his life, Earl wasn't acquainted with the labyrinthine world of police bureaucracy. He hadn't known that such a simple act as retrieving a lone bullet would require endless paperwork—forms that the homeless shelter would fill out for him and file with the Racine Police Department. It was at this juncture that the dynamics began to fall into place for a far more personal drama to develop—one that Earl could never have envisioned when he picked up the bullet from the ground.

Hmm . . . Earl Kloth? an officer in the Racine Police Department wondered, his mind racing, as he happened to randomly pick up the police report detailing the recovery of the live bullet. *Now where have I heard that name before?*

It could have been any police officer in the station

who reviewed the report, but the one who actually did made all the difference in the world. *I know I've heard that name before! . . . Hey, wait a second,* he thought, *didn't someone named Scott Kloth call me about a year ago regarding his search for a long-lost brother? One he had been looking for for thirty years?*

And that is how one lone, stray bullet that other people would have kicked, tossed, or ignored, reunited two brothers in Racine in November 2000. Human nature is such that many of us are quick to deem certain small items as inconsequential, as possessing no real value. But sometimes it is precisely those minuscule items that can lead us to our destiny. Or, at the very least, to a long-lost brother!

By the way, this story has a truly happy ending. Scott convinced Earl to move to Illinois and live with him in his home. Scott even helped Earl get a job working for one of Scott's business partners. "The day he was reunited with his brother, I never saw Earl so happy," said Donna Bumpus, director of the Racine homeless shelter program. "I had never seen him smile so much. It's amazing that what brought these two together was a bullet." ❈

*H*ouses, like people, have auras. Some are cold and uninhabitable. Some are downright evil and forbidding. Then there are those that are warm and welcoming, seeming to envelop you in the spirit of all the life and love that has been lived within their walls.

Such was the case with my grandparents' house. Long the nucleus of many impromptu as well as planned gatherings of family and friends, it was also the home that my long-deceased father lived in as a young man; the home that my recently deceased uncle grew up in; and the home where my dear, beloved Aunt Betty was raised from child to adult. My cousins and I spent much of our own childhoods there as well. There were the Christmas feasts, the huge Sunday dinners, and, of course, the clambakes each summer, which lasted an entire weekend. Needless to say, the house was loved.

The house, located on a prime piece of real estate—a corner lot near several major thoroughfares—had long been a magnet for many ambitious real estate developers.

My grandfather had refused many lucrative offers from several major retail corporations, knowing full well their plans for his castle. To the savvy businessperson, it was not a home filled with life and love and people; it was a piece of land with a building on it that needed to be razed. Literally, to "pave paradise and put up a parking lot."

After the death of my grandfather—and when my grandmother could no longer care for herself and needed to be moved to a long-term health care facility—the bank mandated that the house be put on the market in order for the state to cover her medical expenses.

First there was the auction. Every last dish my grandmother had heaped full of her delectable biscuits and gravy. Every bed on which she had changed the sheets for my young father and aunt to lay their weary bodies on. The wonderful John Deere tractor mower my Poppy had so lovingly tended his corner of the world with.

Gone. It was all gone. Sold off to people who knew only that they'd gotten a bargain. They didn't know the history behind any of it.

It was in this environment that my cousin Cindy decided to throw in her hat and make an offer on the house.

"I just can't see it torn down," she said.

Of course we all felt that way, but she was the only one actually doing something about it.

"What do you think?" she asked me.

"I think you have to try at least. If it was meant to

remain in our family, then it will all work out and your mortgage will come through, and you'll get the house. If it's a place whose time has passed and that should just be left alone with its memories, then you won't, but you'll never know if you don't try. At least you won't spend the rest of your life wondering and what-if-ing yourself to death," I told her.

And so, when the mortgage was approved and Cindy closed on my grandparents' house, no one was more elated than I. Cindy's acquisition of the house meant so much to me that I decided to postpone a cross-country move that I had recently been contemplating. Now I had a reason to stay close to my ancestral roots and I was jubilant. Cindy, however, was still apprehensive.

"I can't believe I'm a homeowner at twenty-six. I don't know if I did the right thing."

But I was sure she had. I would once again be inside that house. That house whose walls nearly spoke to me. That house, which had by now fallen into such a sad state of disrepair that it would take Bob Vila himself a lifetime to restore it to its original glory.

Following Cindy's July 1 closing date, we decided to spend the long July Fourth holiday weekend beginning the seemingly insurmountable task of scraping off layers and layers of ancient paint and wallpaper.

We scraped and we scraped until we thought our arms would break. Cindy was the first one to scrape down to the original plaster walls.

"Look," she said as she revealed the crumbling old dining room wall, "there's something written here. It's a man's name, Howard Doremus."

"Howard Doremus," my Aunt Betty replied. "He's the one who helped us when Mom and Dad first moved in here."

Cindy continued her scraping.

"Wait a minute. There's a date here. July 6, 1949. Isn't that a coincidence?" she said. "Today is July 6, 1997."

And so there we were. Exactly forty-eight years later to the day, we had uncovered a time capsule that a man named Howard Doremus had left for us.

Was my father telling me I was right to have postponed my cross-country move to California? That I was where I needed to be now, for this transition?

Was my grandfather giving Cindy his blessing to fill his home with a whole new generation of Donadio family members?

In any case, we had our answer. We were exactly where we needed to be. Once again, Grandma Sarah and Poppy's house would be filled with life, love, laughter, and noise.

Just the way it always was.

Just the way it was meant to be. ❀

—JANE DONADIO

Even more Small Miracles

Trade paperback, $9.95
ISBN: 1-55850-646-2

Trade paperback, $9.95
ISBN: 1-58062-180-5

Trade paperback, $9.95
ISBN: 1-58062-548-7

Trade paperback, $9.95
ISBN: 1-58062-047-7

Trade paperback, $9.95
ISBN: 1-58062-370-0

The *Small Miracles* series includes five collections of true stories of remarkable coincidences that have changed the lives of ordinary people. These stories, both heartwarming and awe-inspiring, convey that coincidences are more than just random happenings—in fact, they are nothing less than divine messages.

Have you experienced a remarkable
coincidence you want to share?
Go to *www.adamsmedia.com/smallmiracles*
for submission guidelines.

Available Wherever Books Are Sold
For more information, or to order, call 800-872-5627
or visit *www.adamsmedia.com*
Adams Media Corporation, 57 Littlefield Street, Avon, MA 02322.